THE MYSTERY C

The Mystery of Growing Up

Childhood and the Spiritual Life

Practical ideas for parents and teachers

EVELYN FRANCIS CAPEL

TEMPLE LODGE
London

First published in 1960 under the title *Growing Up in Religion* by
The Christian Community Press, London
Reprinted in 1992 by Temple Lodge Press, London

A catalogue record for this book is available from the British Library

ISBN 0 904693 37 6

Printed and bound in Great Britain by
The Cromwell Press Limited, Broughton Gifford, Wiltshire

CONTENTS

Part One

Early Childhood

I

THE SMALL CHILD'S NEED FOR GOD

THE child comes helpless into the world. He starts life with a whole array of needs, for the supplying of which he is dependent on the people around him. His first strong appeal to his parents and others who may be at hand is his need for their care. At no time in later life will he place such complete confidence in others as when, in the first years of his childhood, he entrusts himself, body and soul, to his parents. What a risk is taken at birth! It is no wonder that in their helplessness babies become domestic tyrants demanding that the lives of father and mother be arranged to suit themselves.

On the other hand, the child comes with rich gifts into this world. An atmosphere of sunshine spreads through his home into the hearts of the elder people. Many feelings awaken in them, which they may have forgotten or seem to have lost, such as awe and wonder, trust and hope. As the baby turns into a little child, he makes the everyday world alive and wonderful for his parents. He makes them aware of the wider meaning of simple actions, like giving and taking, walking and jumping, going to sleep and waking up. What is said and done before the child takes on a moral importance, which comes as a shock to many parents. The child's own actions and reactions have a spiritual value out of all proportion to their outer significance. Simple affairs, like sharing out food at a meal, putting on new clothes, saying good-bye or coming home again take on spiritual implications, demanding careful handling. It is advisable to recapture one's own early memories, to become capable of grasping the child's view of life.

It is hard to say who gives more. The child to the parents or the parents to the child. They provide him with the means of living here in a body. He shows them how to illumine this life with the light of the Spirit. They teach him about the world of earth. He recalls to them what they have forgotten about the world of Heaven. How does it come about, one may ask, that helpless babies can give so much to the people round them? However many there are, each one can usually attract a welcome from someone. From whence does the child receive the birthgift which he brings with him from the very first?

The days are passed when it was commonly thought that the child had no existence before the beginnings of the body. The marked character of the newest baby indicates a past history beyond the influences of the hereditary forces given by the parents during the building of the body. In the hearts of those who receive him here the feeling stirs with the coming of the child that an individual person is entering the family. He is bringing his own gifts and powers, his weaknesses and feelings and above all his experience going back into a distant past. He starts life as a person to be reckoned with, to be encountered, to be understood. The child needs to be met with the question, who are you? What do you bring with you?

Contrariwise, small children can be experienced as very much alike, tending to behave in a similar way at the same stages of development. The distinctive character is wrapped up in a sheath of general human nature. The wrapping put round the distinctive individuality is first of all innocence. Later on its common human nature in the shape of the usual capacities for wickedness is added. But the start of every child's life is in innocence. He gives trust before he learns distrust. He knows love before hate, truth before untruth, justice before injustice. He is at one with what is good before he grasps what is bad. Whatever the particular character may be that he brings with him, his being has been impregnated with goodness and innocence before he was born.

Many grown-ups would forget their belief in God, or their experience of the Divine, if it were not for the little children. Divine forces weave around and through them. Their eyes see the world and its inhabitants with divinely inspired sight, which in the course of growing-up becomes dimmed. Some people can still recall this early consciousness in later life, among them a few have been able to put their memories into poetry.

"How like an Angel came I down!
How bright are all things here!
When first among his works I did appear
O how their glory did me crown!
The world resembled His Eternity,
In which my soul did walk;
And everything that I did see
Did with me talk."   (T. Traherne.)

There is an old sacred saying: We are born out of God. Every little child is a living witness that this is a true fact of existence. He brings a portion of the Divine with him as his birthgift and for the first years of his life on earth "Heaven shines about him". The glow of Heaven attracts the older people to be interested in him and to give him their welcome. When the Gate of Birth opens, to let still another soul through, a beam of the divine world-light shines into our present life.

The memory of what being born means for the soul is pictured in most of the traditional fairy stories. Varied as they are, the plot usually follows the same main outline. The story starts with a home, which has to be left behind and a journey taken into a big unknown world. There is a wandering through the forest and over the mountains with strange meetings and situations full of fear and joy. Another type of story opens with a sad plight, a mother dead or a family starving, but a previous good and happy state of affairs is implied. When the child is old enough to appreciate fairy stories, he will recognize a familiar experience within its pictures. In being born there is an element of fear and sadness, an experience of descending from light into darkness. The child's soul has to be consoled for what he is losing by the loving kindness of those who receive him here.

The child needs religion for his healthy development as much as he requires food, sleep and shelter. He comes from the world that is wholly divine into the earthly world, where the divine

9

impress is seen only in the wonders of Nature. He has to make the tremendous change from living, moving and having his being without a body among the forming powers of the universe to inhabiting the bodily house which depends on the laws of physical existence. The child has to learn many facts which he does not know by nature. He has to grasp the difference between day and night, between what is harmful and what is helpful, between his own body and the world around. He is an astonishing contradiction between what he does not know and what he knows already. The difference between the two expresses quite plainly what the existence was like from which he has come. He has to learn about everything that the body obliges him to encounter, but he already knows the realities of the soul.

All human beings from the hour when the body is born until the time when the soul leaves it at death live independent of the will of God. Here on earth we can pray in "The Lord's Prayer", "Thy will be done", because it is not a matter of course that the Divine Will can prevail. In Nature we watch the working of instinctive wisdom which reflects the Divine. Our human behaviour is without such guidance and can freely be as mistaken and self-sufficient as we choose. Our human will is under our own control, because the powers of God abstain from interfering with our impulses. It is hard for us to imagine the sun refusing to shine upon a wrongdoer or a liar falling ill, smitten by his own lies. But should this happen it would reflect the conditions in the world from which we all came at birth. It is natural there that the will of God is all powerful and that here on earth we need to pray that it shall be done.

The child can only understand such a change of existence by degrees. For a long while his natural sense for God lets him see the divine forces at work in the creatures and the people of the world around him. Everything that lives, everything that moves comes straight and wonderful from the hand of God. The people he meets shine with divine qualities, so that he trusts them as long as experience does not teach him otherwise. He has a natural gift for religion because he is all the time aware of the presence of God. When he is older, he will grow out of this state of mind in the course of nature. The world will lose its glow and the clouds of glory will fade. His soul will become lonely and as naturally inclined to sadness as once to happiness. We have all lost something in the process of leaving childhood behind and growing up. But it was real when we had it and need not disappear entirely. The trust in God which we brought with us when we were born should be cherished all through life in the ground of our soul.

The child does not need to be made religious, for that he is already. But the healthy growth of his soul will be hindered if his religious feeling is not protected and encouraged by those who care for him. He should be able to talk about God, to learn about Him and to speak to Him in prayer. The presence of God should be an understood thing between him, his parents and the other older people. The grown-ups, unless they are exceptions in modern times, will feel as if they were receiving a lesson in religion. And, in fact, we all learn from children when it comes to the things of God, because they still live so closely bound up with them. It is tragically wasteful if older people treat this spiritual condition as childish, not to be taken seriously. The child then feels deprived of his most precious gift and is in danger of losing it altogether. If the spirit of the child is quite lost in grown-up people, their powers of thinking, feeling and acting are weakened. They should be able to preserve this treasure of spiritual vitality hidden beneath their adult consciousness.

The child's first need is that his religious life should be recognized and protected. His second need is for words, thoughts and actions to express consciously what he knows in a dream. He is dependent on the people round him for the means of expression. Every child is surrounded by wisdom, but he has to learn how to speak, think and behave from the grown-ups. He cannot bring what he has with him over into his earthly life unless he has the means of transforming it from the unconscious into the conscious. Although he does not need to be taught religion, he wants to be shown how to express what he knows. He will be quite frustrated, if he does not find religiously knowledgeable people who can help him. It is easy to see when a child suffers through lack of food or sleep but harder to understand his spiritual wants.

Those who care for small children can learn how to receive

from them but they have likewise to learn how to give to them. The child's need for God makes demands on the older people, which may require them to look at their own relation to divine things. Then the questions begin: what are the responsibilities of the grown-ups to the small children? Who should look after their religious needs? What preparation and equipment is required?

The first requirement is clearly that which has been spoken of so far, to understand the child's viewpoint as he begins his life here. Mention has been made of the old fairy tales as artistic representations of the experience of coming into this world. In another and more spiritual form the same theme is handled in certain of the parables contained in the New Testament. There is one known as the parable of the talents. It tells of a man of means handing certain sums of money over to his servants as an investment, the amount is in proportion to his estimate of their abilities. Later he calls them to account to find out if the investments have been made to pay. Two have doubled the loans, the third, to avoid risk, has simply left his as it was. He incurs a harsh judgement, while the others receive new opportunities. Each child is born with abilities and opportunities, which are his loan from the Divine World. He has come to increase his power to work for the kingdom of God. Later on he may become ambitious to do well for himself in money and social status. He does not begin with such an outlook, for he is aware of being sent with a spiritual purpose. He expects those who receive him to help him recognize and know what he has brought, that, come what may in this world, he does not bury unprofitably the divine loan.

II

TEACHING RELIGION

WHO is responsible for the religious life of the small child? Put simply, the answer is: Those nearest to him. Who these people are depends in each case on circumstances. The most natural pattern of life places the child in the midst of a family, amongst parents, grandparents, relatives and neighbours. The parents will then feel the first responsibility but they will not be alone. Most young children learn quickly and easily from grandparents. Much can be gained from looking back into one's own childhood and reviewing the people who played an important part at that time. There will be many to whom we should be grateful, a grand-mother who told stories and who prayed, a grandfather, who had done something in life and was wise from experience, an enter-prising aunt, a gallant uncle, a neighbour who knew strange things about plants and insects, another, who could handle tools. The list would in reality be much longer. It would start with mother and father, who whether or no they will, have the most decisive influence on the child's religious life.

The parents encounter the religious needs of their child from the first moment that they are aware of his existence. That will be before he is born, as soon as they realize that he is on his way to them. Religion is a much bigger element in human life than is often imagined nowadays by those who say: What do I believe, what shall I teach my child, what church shall we attend? or shall we leave the whole problem and let him decide for himself what he wants to believe when he is grown-up? Our whole human life is related in all its parts to our connection with the Divine, that is, to religion. For a while it has been a social custom to treat it as a thing apart from other affairs, to be dealt with at special times like Sunday morning, and in special places, like the church or chapel. A person could be fitted out with a religion as part of his general equipment for decent living.

In earlier times quite different customs prevailed. Every aspect of human affairs was interwoven with religious practice. The seasons of the year were marked by church festivals and the times of the day were counted by the ringing of the church bell for prayer. Every activity of life was dedicated in its own way to God and on every undertaking His blessing was evoked. Man's life was felt to be carried in the hand of God, and so bound to prosper in every part through true religion. Grown-up people are nowadays less convinced of their dependence on the Divine World, but children still experience this state of existence. It is unnatural for them to cut any part of life off from religion.

The parents' outlook on the world begins to influence the child as his soul approaches the earth. He is affected particularly in the strength or weakness of his confidence in life. The attitude of his father and mother to the things of the Spirit will work upon his approach to existence on earth. If they have a real faith in God, even a vague one, it will help him to have faith in his purpose here. If they are willing to inquire into the spiritual facts of the world and to understand them for themselves, he will receive satisfying answers to his early questions and increased strength in his will to grow up and contribute his share to Man's future. Should they have learnt, for instance, some insight into the patterns that form themselves in the life-stories of men and women, they will know how divine influences work in human affairs. Many of the events, which we encounter through the years, we have planned ourselves or brought about by our own doings. Others come to us from quite beyond ourselves bringing great good fortune or great tragedy, for which we cannot see the cause. Decisive changes of destiny can be traced to those events in which a higher will than our own is at work. The wisdom of God intervenes to shape our lives. Whoever is able to understand this reality, will be a helpful guide to little children starting out in life.

It is possible to take a further step in knowledge. We can observe the working of divine forces in human destinies. But forces depend on beings from whom they stream out and who are working through them. We hear footsteps in the distance. We recognize the sound of moving feet. We then inquire who it is walking along the road. We can say likewise that where divine forces can be felt, divine beings, instruments of the will of God, are at work. Whoever can go to this length, can look at himself or another person with the conviction that he has a guardian angel, whose appointed and hard task it is to protect his higher being from harm and watch over his true welfare. Such a one will give to a child great assistance in overcoming his natural fear of life.

Are children intended to take their parents as they find them and to adapt themselves to their ways? Or should parents prepare themselves for the needs of the children, even if they should then have to take a different interest in religious matters than they did earlier? If the needs of the children are to be the first consideration, fathers and mothers have to prepare themselves spiritually for parenthood. They will not require in the early years a set of doctrines, but an attitude to life inspired by religious feeling and understanding. The capacity to show respect is the first essential requirement for such an attitude.

"The world is so full of a number of things
I'm sure we should all be as happy as kings."
(R. L. Stevenson)

The ground is firm under our feet, and supports us in all our doings. The plants and trees grow up, change with the seasons, bear leaves, blossom and fruit in due time. The birds fly and sing, the fishes glide and swim, the animals leap and run, are hungry and feed, make lairs and bring up their young. If we forget the continual wonder of these things, the world turns stale. When we try to experience it again and again our eyes are opened to see what is divine in creation, in all that is around, above and below. As our insight increases so our respect develops for all that it is given us to see, to receive and to handle. Under modern conditions, it is necessary to pay attention to all that we have to do, plan and carry out ourselves by our own enterprise. We have to make our way in the world. It requires an effort to look at the other side and realize how much is given to us by the unseen hand of God and by the divine impulses of loving kindness and care in the people we encounter. From such considerations the respect awakens in the heart towards all that is part of life. Feeling of this nature can be refreshed by listening to certain passages in the Bible, in the Old Testament, to the Psalms and the Book of Job. They sing the wonderful works of God with a vigour refreshing to our careworn minds today.

Through feelings of respect and wonder to all that is around, we are in natural sympathy with little children, who know these before any others. It is not necessary to tell them about this attitude to life but they require that we shall show it to them in our behaviour. From the child's point of view the grown-ups should know how to be religious in all their actions and doings, by handling the simplest and most ordinary affairs with respect for the divine forces in all creatures and things. Most people have to prepare themselves to be able to do this, not on special occasions but in the bustle of everyday. The child is given a drink from a cup, or food from a spoon. He is receiving what he is taking from the living abundance of Nature, at the hand of his mother or another person who realizes his need for nourishment and his dependence on herself. One day he offers the cup or the spoon to the one who is feeding him. The style in which he makes the gesture will reflect the attitude in the hearts and actions of those who have been looking after him. Later on he will begin to enjoy feeding birds and animals and being allowed to help older people in what they are doing. In the apparently small actions of living he is finding his relationship to the world around in receiving and giving. The children of parents with little or no religious feeling will go through the same stages of natural development as those with fathers, mothers and grandparents, who can show respect and reverence. But the behaviour they learn and the forces of heart they express will later show the difference. Our whole relationship to life and to other people is in reality an expression of our understanding of God. Those who see the world empty of the Divine will see a bare material place in which to exercise their cleverness and their instinctive longings in competition with other people, who are doing likewise. Those who have insight into the working of God's will meet His image in other men and women and recognize His wisdom informing and inspiring the creatures of the earth. They will be able to respect wisdom and feel compassion. They will be known by their behaviour.

The young child soon wishes to think and to talk about God, to ask questions about His working, and to hear of His interest in our human sayings and doings. The childish remarks may seem over-practical but children are by nature not yet able to separate the spiritual from the physical in the manner of grown-ups. They should be taken seriously and in good faith, although it is not easy to be imaginative enough to answer rightly in the same style. The grown-ups will need to have given thought to their picture of God in advance if the children are not to be disappointed by having their questions put off or being made to suffer by having them rejected altogether. If a child wants to speak of his guardian angel, about where he himself lived before he was born, about what happens when he is asleep, he expects that all those around him will have thought of such things and be able to understand them. He wants to learn by getting hold of earthly thoughts and words but he expects to make his own serious contribution to such conversations. He is shocked to be considered childish and amusing or to be met with ignorance and unbelief.

The earliest instruction given to children will be mostly in the form of answers to questions. They are likely to be asked suddenly, without warning, when the parents or other grown-ups are thinking of something different. Those who have a little time to give to the children between the moments of their going to bed and falling asleep, will find out the special quality of this interval between day and night. A little serious talking on both sides comes more easily than at any other time. A difficult question can sometimes be saved up till then from an inconvenient moment, if it is a family custom to have a little leisure at bedtime. But how should the questions be tackled, when they come? What does it mean to be honest with children? Many a parent says to himself: at least I will not tell the child what I do not believe myself. Certainly no one should tell untruths to children, and it is indeed useless to make the attempt even for good reasons. They have the gift in the early years of listening through what is said to that

17

which lies behind. They realize spontaneously if something is being said for effect or on principle. They can distinguish truth from untruth with a clarity which they unfortunately do not keep in their later years. But they do not understand or even tolerate willingly arguments or uncertainties. A straight answer to a straight question sums up the expectations of the small child. Discussion about belief and not belief puts a strain upon him for which he is quite unprepared until he is older.

It is not enough for parents to fall back on the principle of not saying anything that they do not believe. They should have provided themselves with positive beliefs or understanding to be ready for the questions when they come. It is just as harmful to give no answer as to give an untrue one. But due allowance should be made for the difference in consciousness between the mind of the child and of the grown-up. An incomprehensible answer is no answer. The child thinks in pictures, which he takes for reality. The world around gives him pictures continually and he reads moral and spiritual meanings in natural things. The mind of the grown-up has separated the natural from the spiritual, the wisdom in Nature from the moral understanding and judgement within the soul, the outer from the inner. The child does not make this distinction. He shares the experience which historically can be found among the ancient Greeks, reflected in their use of language. They had the same word "pneuma" for spirit and for wind, because they felt them to be identical. Those who translate the Gospels into modern English encounter these Greek nouns of double meaning as hindrances. Modern people distinguish the outer from the inner by using different words, except in childhood when the earlier and older consciousness prevails. The child thinks and experiences in pictures to which he gives a literal interpretation. He can comprehend ideas of the widest and deepest meaning, if they reach him pictorially. It is not necessary to cut down thoughts for the sake of his mind, as his clothes are made small to fit his body. He will become impatient with small conceptions. But he comprehends in pictures and the grown-ups need to exert all their power of imagination and more to express themselves adequately in this style.

The child should be able to realize that he experiences the

18

presence of God in the stones, plants and animals, in everything that lives and moves. Thomas Traherne, the first lines of whose poem on his own childhood have already been quoted, says in a later verse:

"The skies in their magnificence
  The lively lovely air,
Oh how divine, how soft, how sweet, how fair!
  The stars did entertain my sense,
And all the works of God, so bright and pure,
  So rich and great did seem,
  As if they ever must endure
    In my esteem."

He should see the image of God likewise in his father and mother, his grandparents, and all the people, big and little, whom he encounters. One day, at a later stage, he will start to notice the weakness and poverty in other people but in his first period of life he is shown a vision like this:

"The streets were paved with golden stones
  The boys and girls were white,
O how did all their lovely faces shine!
  The sons of men were holy ones
In joy and beauty they appeared to me
And everything which here I found
  While like an Angel I did see,
    Adorned the ground."   (Traherne)

There is no need to fear that the child is under an illusion. The angel's viewpoint is just as real and valid as that of the cynical adult. The child is given the gift of seeing what is divine in the world, to which he has just come before he sees the opposite. The grown-ups will show him how to come down to earth and he will shed amongst them the light of his insight into the Divine.

Story-telling is another form which instruction takes in the lives of young children. The earliest ones, suitable for a number of years, will be about the things of Nature, about plants and trees, streams and hills, birds and beasts, insects and fishes. They should be very simple until the child himself, out of his own development, demands that they should be more complex. It is often difficult to adjust the mind of the grown-up to the child's delight in very simple events. The tales should be imaginative but true to reality, avoiding for instance animals dressed in human clothes, busy with shopping and cooking. The being and character of the creatures themselves should be expressed, the difference between the cow, the sheep, the dog and the cat is interesting, while all animals are a dead loss turned into sham people by the story-teller. An excellent plot for a child's story goes something like this. A little boy goes into a forest. One by one a group of different beasts gather in a clearing. Each one shows the boy what he can do better than all the others. Finally the animals ask the boy to show them what he can do, which they cannot. He sadly says that the only thing that he can do is to laugh but they all answer that they would rather be able to laugh than anything else.

Stories from Nature can be found in books or invented by the story-tellers, who will easily discover from the child listener himself what does or does not find response. The purpose of the stories is not to teach natural history, which is desirable at a much later age, but to reveal the soul life in Nature. All such stories have in reality the same theme, to show the working of God in all that lives, moves and has its being around us. It will be necessary in the later stage of early childhood to include stories of the soul life of human beings. The presence of God within them should be illustrated again and again.

Correct timing is very important in the upbringing of children. The trend of today often produces in grown-ups too great an anxiety to push the child quickly from one stage of development to the next and to let him have experiences too soon. By early childhood is meant here the years between birth and the change of teeth, which usually occurs between six and seven years old. The child will require more imaginative stories in the latter portion of this period and they will be fairy stories and fables. There is a rich variety of fairy stories from all nations of the world offering the story-teller a wide choice. They are not at all fantastic, if they are in the true tradition, because they express an inner meaning in outer pictures. They speak of the experience of the human soul. Each figure represents different parts in the character of one human being. The princess and the prince, the good mother and the wicked stepmother, the faithful servant are not separate people but elements within the soul of each person. What they experience in the story are the inner changes the child passes through in coming down to earth, growing-up, coming to terms with his own forces and capacities and finding his destiny. Fairy stories describe the drama of the human soul living between Heaven and earth. Children understand them imaginatively by their own inner wisdom, if they have them at the most suitable age, that is to say, after the simple stories about the creatures of Nature. Then they require fables describing the inner character of animals and fairy stories illustrating the inner life of human beings.

Bible stories are for the most part required in the development of the child at the next stage, beginning after the seventh year. We learn about God not only from the Bible but from life itself, which should be the small child's holy book. On special occasions he may want a glimpse into what is to come, as when he hears of Mary and the Christ-child at Christmastime. On the whole, he is better saved from hearing everything too soon or having great stories cut down to small size. It is a problem of developing consciousness. Fairy stories represent a stage in the growth of the mind through which the child passes just before and after the changing of the teeth. In his way he will learn from them of the working of God in the human soul.

Religious instruction is part of the small child's home life. It is not a matter to be dealt with by calling in the clergyman or the expert. The first who teach the child about divine things are as a matter of course, his parents, his grandparents, his friends. When they find themselves undertaking this responsibility, they will discover that it brings with it a natural reward. They become aware that their daily behaviour, the answers they give to questions, the stories they tell instruct the child and themselves at the same time in the wisdom-filled ways of God.

III

THE CHILD AT PRAYER

WHEN should the child begin to pray? He should have prayer from the very beginning of his life, as soon as he hears human speech. Prayer is divine conversation, for which the capacities of listening, thinking and speaking are used at their highest value. From the hour of his birth onwards the baby listens to what is said around him, learning from older people what it means to talk. His whole being listens with eager interest to the sounds and forms of language, absorbing them into himself, preparing for the time when he will be able to speak as well as to hear. He will have his first lessons in prayer when he listens to his father and mother and other people praying. He will experience that the power of speech is holy, that it is rightly used for men to speak to God. He will absorb the knowledge that a divine element lives in man's being, giving him the right to pray and the power to speak, which he alone has among all the creatures on earth. In the act of praying a human being expresses the true dignity of himself. The child should have the opportunity to witness it and learn from it.

"The first impressions are Immortal all" (Traherne). Perhaps in modern times it is necessary to qualify this saying from the seventeenth century with the word "should be" in place of "are". Those who care for little children see from experience what intense devotion they show to all impressions received from the world and the people around them. Is it not then part of the care they require to provide them with some experiences of a high, even of a sacred order? A simple experiment can be carried out by a parent or nurse with a baby in charge. At the end of the day a review can be made of all the conversations and sounds that the child will have heard for the last twelve hours. He will have absorbed them all into his inner nature and they will already be influencing his speaking and thinking for later years. Has he only heard words slurred and badly pronounced? Has he listened to only trivial and careless talk? Has he also had quiet and heard the silence? If the radio was on all day, if people only spoke of superficial things in his company, his opportunity of developing later a musician's feeling for music, a poet's sense of language, a religious man's thought for the values in life has been hindered. The baby and the little child absorb all that they see and hear into the deep part of their constitution. In the first years much of their "second nature" for later life is built into them.

How can the earliest influences be good and helpful ones? The child's experiences can be very simple and should not be overwhelming. A mother or father singing at his bedside, or someone playing a simple tune on a pipe will mean very much to him, even if their performance is not expert, while classical music would be overpowering. The stories he hears can be simple, the poems can be nursery rhymes. But they should be told and sung with devotion to the way a human being can use his powers of singing, speaking and thinking. There is no method of helping a child in his early life except by the people round him becoming aware that they themselves should show him what it means to be human. In the highest sense he learns from them how man is made in the image of God. So he will receive his first training for worthy manhood in the years to come. When he is older, after he has reached school age, experts can be found to teach him what the people at home have not learnt. But in the first years he depends on those nearest to him to be as expert as they know how in the art of being human. Someone who does not pray is not living properly as a human being. Prayer therefore should be one of the experiences of childhood.

The child's day follows a natural rhythm according to his physical needs at each stage of growth. Two moments stand out at all ages with special significance, going to sleep at night and waking up in the morning. It is a naturally right feeling that the day should begin and end with prayer. Before the child can speak himself, his mother or his father, or both together, should say a prayer beside him on his behalf. When he is able to start saying the words himself, he will join in, most likely of his own accord. One day he may want, demand or be encouraged to say them alone. But for a long time, until he reaches his teens perhaps, he will want one or both of his parents to be present and to listen to him. Until his natural development leads him to wish for the privacy of his own thoughts, prayer should be shared with his parents, his brothers and sisters, the whole family. Everything important will be shared in the early years, and prayer will be no exception.

A careful organization of the family life will be required to make and keep the custom of morning and evening prayer. No one is likely to succeed unless its high importance has been thoroughly grasped. Most people today are not religious by tradition. They have to think the whole matter out afresh for themselves and form their customs accordingly. But conviction of the need for prayer increases in everyone who gives thought to the mystery of his own human existence. When we fall asleep at night, we hand ourselves over to forces of which we know very little and over which we have no control. We leave the shore of our conscious existence and set out over an unknown sea, until, by a will greater than our own, we are brought back again. We return with vital forces renewed and refreshed and, if we observe carefully enough, with a wider outlook and a calmer wisdom of mind. If we give real thought to the mystery of sleep, we begin to realize that our souls have been in another sphere than that we know by day, from which we bring back gifts like those the child is endowed with at birth. We have visited the realms of God again. By contrast, while we are awake during the day, we are conscious of ourselves, of our actions, our problems, our hopes. We set about the business of life out of our own known powers. Awake we act on our own responsibility; asleep we give ourselves over to the divine forces of the universe. Is it not naturally a proper thing to pray at each transition from one of these contrasting states of existence to the other?

The further question arises of how the child should be taught to behave at prayer-time. It is good to let the saying of the prayer be the last event before kissing good night and settling down. This implies that much will have gone before. All the affairs of undressing and going to bed will be over, the playing about and

24

the quietening down. A little time will have been taken over a story or the consideration of a question that may have arisen during the day. Some short singing is a good introduction to the actual prayer. On the other hand, in some families the mother may prefer to sing alone, as the children are going off to sleep. When the prayer is said, the outer behaviour is very important, the more so the younger the child. In the first stage of life, little distinction is felt between soul and body, between inner experience and outer impression. A child kneels from reverence, while an older person can be just as reverent sitting or even lying down. In earlier times of history, people remained at all ages more as children are now. Chairs were not provided then in churches, and still are not in some countries today. Praying without kneeling down or standing up was unthinkable. The outer actions of kneeling, folding the hands and shutting the eyes meant prayer, as they still do for the child. The words should be spoken as clearly and solemnly as possible. Some occasions of quiet dignity are necessary in the life of the child, who can appreciate them out of himself. If he is otherwise given enough opportunity to romp and play, he will be grateful for the different experience of being quiet and solemn, if it does not last too long. He does not always want to be childish and feels hampered if he is expected to be.

The other occasion for prayer is the beginning of the day. It may be difficult to achieve under modern conditions, but before the ordinary affairs begin, a prayer should be said. But it need not demand much actual time. When the whole procedure, for instance, of going to bed is described, it sounds altogether too lengthy. In fact no one item need last long for the small child. A story told for five to ten minutes is long at the age when time goes slowly, as it does early in life. A song or hymn of two verses provides sufficient singing. The prayer itself should be short. The value of the bedtime procedure for the child lies in the rhythmical repetition. As regularly as the sun sets and rises, the prayers should be said even in times of sickness and trouble or of change and excitement. Value is also attached by the child to each separate item being included, providing him with the variety of experience he needs. Both these considerations are much more important than the amount of time actually expended.

Other occasions for prayer during the day may arise from special events, which, for people to whom praying is a real experience and not a convention, call for prayer. In one family of small children, the three elder ones were told that a new little sister had arrived. They said to each other: we must pray for baby, and all knelt down without further ado, quite undisturbed by the circumstance that they happened to be in the back of a car at the time. Children brought up so that the prayer is a natural and proper part of life, without artificial piety, can behave in such a manner. If we speak to God before starting upon the activities and excitements of the day, should we not all the more pray for a baby whose first day of life has dawned? Should we not likewise be able to pray before doing something which needs our best powers? The mediaeval monks who wrote by hand and illustrated with painting and drawing the words of the Gospels and the Psalms, the stonemasons who carved the designs and pictures for the walls of the old cathedrals made a habit of saying a prayer as they took up their tools for a fresh session of work. They were not calling on divine power to come and do their job for them. They were offering their ability and skill to God that His power might unite with theirs that work of the Spirit might be fulfilled on earth.

Mealtimes are the occasion for saying grace, that is to say for a particular kind of prayer. Everyone needs food and no one can have it entirely by his own efforts. It must be grown, gathered, transported, shopped for, prepared, cooked and served. Most modern people can only carry out a small part of this process for themselves and for the remainder, they depend on others. But should an exceptional person grow and gather part of his food from his own land, he is still not doing everything for himself. The production of food depends on what comes from the earth below and from the sky above to weave together in the processes of growth. When we eat, realizing what we are doing, we acknowledge our need for food and the divine forces of the world, which it contains, that is to say, we say grace. By recognizing that the world gives us nourishment, we become more awake to what other people contribute to our meals. We acknowledge that we are grateful to the forces of God and the work of others. Whatever form of words are chosen for the grace, they should rightly express two facts of life. They should be a reminder that food is produced by the unseen processes that take place between Heaven and earth. They should awaken the thought that nourishment is a gift by which we, having received, will have the strength to give. Little children, who eat after having said grace, will not take for granted what is given to them. They will experience in themselves the power to give thanks and to give help.

The question of what forms of prayer are to be used by the small child depends on the choice of the parents or other people around him. They will wish to combine two points of view. They will look for thoughts in the prayers, in which they can believe wholeheartedly themselves, but for forms of expression which suit the child's different kind of consciousness. It should be stressed once more that children are not childish over serious matters. By their own wish they will speak about profound ideas but they should not be forced into an adult cast of mind. A boy once wrote at six years old in his diary: "photograph the devil but do not look at the photograph too often." The thought is as deep and true as any that he could have as a grown-up person and he has found his own most happy way of expressing it. He is aware of the devil, a real being whose measure has to be taken. He will recognize the being of God in the same realistic manner and expect to pray with the same directness.

The child's realization of God is more simple and straight-forward than that of the grown-ups. He has not reached the age of doubts and discussions. He feels the living being in himself, he is aware of the same in other people, he watches the changing life in the plants and animals and knows that everywhere in them all is the presence of God. This idea should be the theme of prayers for children because it lives in their own experience. Grown-ups, with their more abstract ways of thinking, are farther away from it, but can recognize its truth after their own fashion. The practical question, how is the idea to be expressed in words of prayer which the child can repeat, will be left open here, to avoid suggestions which restrict the parents' personal choice. One point, however, may be added. There is a distinction between saying: "God made me" and "God is in me". The first expresses the power of God but puts Him away from and above me, taking all authority and responsibility to Himself. The second sentence approaches the same fact from the other direction. God is not far off and apart from me. His Spirit moves in me and in others. His wisdom and His will can work in and through me. I am here on earth, in myself, part of His divine existence. This second thought can bring the sense of direction so much needed when choosing prayers.

A second necessary part of prayer is that it brings renewed trust and confidence in God. The first stage in praying is to be aware of and acknowledge the divine presence. Only so can the heart be lifted up towards the Divine World. But the impulse to pray contains the longing for an answer to a request. What kind of request can rise from the heart of a child to God? The child is growing every day further and further into his earthly nature. He faces new experiences in the world, new meetings with people and things, new demands in himself. In the experience of childhood he lives with the contrast between the fear of what he encounters and the love to all that meets him. Fear drags him into the darkness, love lets him walk in the light. Fear weakens the soul, love strengthens it. In fear he knows the power of the devil, in love the power of God. At later stages of development more complicated experiences will arise in the soul, but the original theme of life in the early years is the struggle to overcome fear and the longing to grow in love. The child's heart lifts itself in prayer for strength against fear and for power to love to the Spirit of God. Whatever form of words may be chosen, the prayer should be such that this essential request is made. Every prayer said by a child needs, because childhood is what it is, two ingredients, the presence of God recognized in each human being and in the creatures of the world and the request made for the power of love.

What of other requests? Should the old formula be repeated: God bless mother, father and everyone? What is to be thought of requests to receive something much wanted or to be spared something very unpleasant? Such questions apply at all ages of life, but when it comes to teaching a child how to pray, they have to be faced in all their consequences. The religious life brings with it one temptation more than others, egotism. When people turn to God for what they hope to get, comfort, a sense of security, uplifting emotions or personal wishes made to come true, their selfishness falls between themselves and Him. "Thy ways are higher than my ways and Thy thoughts than my thoughts." These words from the Bible describe the state of mind which is necessary to true prayer. There is all the difference between presenting God with a list of requirements and lifting up the heart to ask that the light of Divine Wisdom shine upon our ways and those of our loved ones. The child should be protected from losing his natural reverence for the greatness of God and from slipping into the habit of making selfish requests.

If this condition is fulfilled it is natural and good to pray for all those we love and for all who need help. The loving warmth of our hearts may be offered to God that it may be united with His wisdom and so stream to them on the beams of His light. When we begin to think in prayer of those for whom we wish to pray, we make an inner picture of them, and if they are especially in need, of the plight in which they are. We offer these pictures up with our feelings of love for them. In this form of asking it becomes unnecessary to tell God what should be done for them ourselves. Instead of that, we offer our picture, as it were, for His consideration, bringing the souls of those whom we love before Him, that we may stand together in His sight. Such an attitude cannot be explained to a small child but he will feel it from the manner in which he is taught to pray for other people. He will not be tempted to start asking for what he wants for himself, if he can pray for others in this way. The old sentence beginning "God bless" is still beautiful if it is used selflessly, but before the child can put it to good use, the grown-ups will need to have given thought to what it means. There was a time long ago, when there was no need to explain the word "bless" with its opposite "curse". When these words were used then, the results were immediately seen. Someone who had been cursed, shrivelled in soul as if under a bad spell. He felt himself becoming smaller, weaker and more miserable. By contrast, someone who was blessed, expanded in his whole being like a flower in sunshine. He felt his soul strengthened and uplifted, his burdens and his sorrows eased and lightened. Nowadays the use of the word has become a vague expression of goodwill but it can be revived with careful thought for what a blessing should mean. The children cannot do this themselves but they can learn to say the word from grown-ups who are trying to give it again living reality. By asking God to bless others in this sense, they will grow into people who are later able to give blessing themselves by their own human presence.

When we pray, we recognize that we walk along the road of life from the beginning to the end in the presence of God. The little child has come so lately into the dark place of this world that he can turn back spontaneously to the well-remembered Divine Light. He can say his prayers as a joyful act, turning back to Him from whom he was sent. This thought was once put into poetry by Thomas Traherne from whose writings quotations have already been made.

> "From God above
> Being sent, the Heavens me enflame.
> To praise His Name
> The stars do more!
> The burning sun doth shew His love.
> O how divine
> Am I! To all this sacred wealth,
> This life and health,
> Who raised? Who mine
> Did make the same? What hand divine?"

IV

MORAL TRAINING

"O THAT is naughty! Now be a good child." How soon such words are heard after the child is born will vary with everyone, but come they will and sooner than might be expected. The child lives between his wishes and fears and the approval and disapproval of the people around him. He starts life with great powers of will which cause his little limbs to move and forces of feeling, of like and dislike, which impel him to smile and cry. His thinking develops later, as he learns at the same time to walk and to talk. His earliest experiences are the impact of his will upon the surroundings and their reaction to him. He learns the words "good" and "naughty" according to whether his behaviour strikes the people round him favourably or not. Such is his first introduction to moral problems.

At the beginning of life the distinction between outer and inner, between psychological and physical, between soul and body is not yet developed. Behaviour is everything in the first years but in the process of growing up the distinction gradually becomes a matter of experience. Those who bring up children need plentiful imagination to help assist this development. They need to find the right transition from regulating behaviour to pursuing the question of motives. If the child's awareness of his motives is awakened too soon he can be over-burdened with a hampering sense of guilt, which he will later resent. Or his intelligence will be too soon directed towards himself and he will become sly, playing upon the feelings of the grown-ups instead of trusting them. If, on the other hand, he is too long judged by behaviour only, his inner moral sense will stay asleep after it should have awakened. His judgements will become superficial in later years and he will be satisfied to conform to what the people around him expect. Instead of becoming a morally active person, he will simply accept passively or rebel against the standards of others.

Much rebellious behaviour in youth arises from reaction against parents who were themselves unable to make the transition in their treatment of the child.

The words "good" and "naughty" heard before the child can speak or understand, will convey to him by the tone in which they are said, the first experience of moral judgements. Even if some parents would try not to use these actual words, they would still, as a matter of course, dispense to their child praise and blame which comes to just the same thing. It is part of their business as mothers and fathers to do so, for the new-comer to this world cannot find his way unless he receives their directions. He learns from them how to deal with the affairs of the body, how to behave in domestic life, how to eat at mealtimes, to sleep at night, to dress on getting up, to undress on going to bed. He is not born knowing the things of everyday, he has to be taught. Likewise he has to learn how to conduct himself in matters of the soul. He is possessed from the start of a treasure of innocence and goodness, a living substance of morality within him. How this shall flow into his behaviour in an earthly sense, he still has to learn from the older more experienced people round about. As he grows older, bigger and cleverer, he will discover how to be selfish. He will need help in recognizing and restraining the urges to wickedness that beset earthly human nature. Again he will need the help and direction given by the praise and blame of the grown-ups.

The child, at bottom, relies on his parents to be severe with him at the right moments and does not resent their power to blame and punish. But parents have not always given enough consideration to their rights over their offspring before they start using them. They might even be surprised themselves, if they heard objectively what they say and how they speak. An important distinction can be recognized in the use of the words "good" and "naughty". It is quite one thing to say, "you are a naughty child" and quite another to say, "what you are doing is naughty". The child easily recognizes that he has to learn how to behave, but he can be hurt and resentful, if he feels himself accused of being bad. He can be shocked and discouraged to be blamed as a person, when he can accept as justified disapproval for what he has done. He expects to reach an understanding with

32

the grown-ups on matters of behaviour, over which they have a natural right to judge, but to keep himself to himself as a person with his own dignity. Misunderstandings between a child and his parents or other relatives frequently arise from confusion between what he does and what he is. He will benefit from tactful handling and the right measure of tact is to be found by realizing as a grown-up this distinction, of which he is always aware. A child's dignity of person is very precious to him.

Another necessary distinction is that between childish actions that are really worthy of blame and those that are simply inconvenient to the grown-ups. Little children do not grasp how tired, worried and short of time older people can be. Sometimes they have a strong feeling for the welfare of others before they can even speak, and, in a spirit beyond their years, undertake to feed the hungry and clean up the dirt with inconvenient consequences. A hasty grown-up, who has not paused to observe what the little person was really intending, may do great harm by an unthinking reaction. An even worse situation comes about when mother and father continually make their own likes, dislikes and convenience into the standards of right and wrong for the whole family. It then becomes more important not to make father angry than not to do something selfish. The respect for the moral judgement of the parents is effectively undermined, although the children may outwardly conform.

Parents have natural moral authority over children throughout childhood. Grandparents may share it, nursemaids may have a portion delegated to them, teachers will later on have an authoity of their own. But the first principle in moral training will unavoidably be authority. Where the grown-ups are afraid to exercise it and try to avoid responsibility by letting the children do as they like, their weakness will produce a bitter harvest in later years. The substance of authority is the power to praise and to blame, to reward and to punish. An impersonal sense of justice is the first requirement for exercising it well. Children start life with a fine sense of what is just and unjust. "It isn't fair" is one of their readiest complaints. They appreciate strictness as long as it is impartial. People, who give great thought to problems of upbringing, will often be very concerned about what they should and should not do, whether to demand obedience from the children or not, whether to smack them or not. These are in reality not the important questions. They will solve themselves through the sense of justice of the parents, when it is combined with sufficient imagination in matters of right and wrong.

The moral experiences of small children arise from behaviour. The grown-ups uphold the standards and judge the consequences of what the children do and say. When the children have understood and accepted the standards, they will accept punishment as part of the consequences. In later years it will be advisable to discuss and explain wrongdoing, but if this is done too early in life, it will cause intellectual strain and confusion. Small children understand best punishment that is a prompt result of judgement and reaction on the part of the grown-ups. If someone does not look where he is going, he falls down and hurts himself, if he runs into a tree, he bumps his head. The world around has reacted with consequences to his actions. The grown-ups are to small children part of the world around them whose business it is to produce moral consequences. If a child is smacked in this style, it will not harm him. If he is made to help clear up the mess, he will be convinced. A delayed punishment, a talking-to much later, a series of rebukes from different people will burden him with too much guilt. If he is made to feel a nuisance or a cause of unhappiness, he will begin to mistrust his relationship to the family and be afraid.

In his early years the child is very sensitive to the feelings and thoughts of the people round him. He does not need to be told what is in their hearts, nor does he listen to their words as much as to the tone and mood of what they say. At the same time he cannot shut himself off from what is passing through their soul life as an older more self-centred person might. It often comes as a shock to a grown-up to find out how strongly a child reflects and reacts to his state of mind. The reaction is far from being always that of sympathy. The hurried, worried grown-up will provoke a child to be slow and obstinate. The anxious tearful person can make a child cross and hard-hearted. A tragic situation may cause him to retreat into himself and appear quite unfeeling because he is overwhelmed. But however contradictory his behaviour, he is always deeply concerned with the feelings of all those around him. It is therefore a big part of his moral training to feel what he rouses in them by his words and actions. The punishment is aftermath compared with the drama of emotion of which he has become the centre. The grown-ups do well to estimate the effect of the situation on the child's feeling before they calculate the appropriate reaction. It may be necessary to say and do very little in fact. Their activity has a strong backing in the morally sensitive nature of the child. In the first period of life he will never question that their feeling for what he has said and done is right, unless they themselves undermine his confidence. He believes the world to be just and his parents to represent justice and truth. Is this because he is inexperienced? It is rather the other way round. He comes into this world experienced in the ways of the Divine World. He looks here for the reflection of what he knows already. He was used to the presence of God. Now his parents have taken God's place and for the first years of his life here, he will expect them to fill it. He will hold them responsible for maintaining the rightness of things, in this world, as the divine order is upheld in the realms from which he has come.

The authority of the older people is the first means of moral training in early childhood, but the second, of equal importance, is the child's ability to imitate. Little children learn busily all through the years before they attend school. They learn how to develop their capacities of body and mind and how to deal with the circumstances of this earthly world. A few minutes spent picturing to oneself what a baby and a toddler are experiencing and developing in the course of one day will leave behind the impression that never in later years does someone learn so much so quickly as in the first six of his life. Small children are intensely occupied trying to sit up, stand, walk, run and control their limbs. At the same time they are turning shouts and cries into properly formed words and sentences and making concepts of what they find around and within themselves. They are learning the business of daily life, how to deal with the objects and the jobs necessary to maintain it. In addition they are receiving and digesting experience, by playing back to themselves in games

35

what they have seen and heard. It is useful to observe what shows itself when the children play on their own and repeat what they have absorbed. One becomes convinced that it is a full-time job to be a small child. The capacity by which so much development is achieved in so short a time is imitation as a means of learning and it is most intensively active in the first years of life.

The child imitates what he finds around him. Much strength can be wasted on the wearisome business of saying "don't" or trying to demand obedience by threats, which could be saved by appealing to the impulse to copy what is done by someone at hand. From the small child's own point of view, he does not expect to do what he is told, but to reflect what he sees. The main concern of those who bring him up, will be to watch carefully over his experiences and over their own behaviour. He is modelling his sayings and doing on theirs. If they wish him to become an honest, truthful and hardworking person, he should see these virtues first in them. If they are selfish, lazy and careless, he will learn to copy the same attitude to life. He will be watching them with the penetrating eye of the very young, who do not see excuses or special circumstances. Father may be tired, mother hard-pressed, but the child's attention is on the careless action or the irritable expression. Inevitably those who train children train themselves in self-observation and self-control. If they get exasperated or impatient, the unhappy moment comes when they find themselves blaming the little ones for behaving in a way that they have learnt from their example. Such a piece of injustice is keenly felt. The fact of the matter is that moral education goes on at both ends simultaneously. It is hard to say who is teaching whom more, the grown-ups the child or the child the people round him.

It is easier to accept the principle that a good example should be set, than to realize in practice how literal is the interpretation put on every action by the childish mind. A little girl was heard to say to her mother who was gossiping to a neighbour about mutual friends: "Mother, which of your friends do you dislike most?" Criticism, perhaps not too good-natured, could only mean dislike or hate to the small girl. In fact, to criticize other people in front of a young child, causes him to begin despising instead of respecting those around him. It is of no use for them to demand his respect for themselves later on, for they have taught him how to be disrespectful by their own example, although they may have meant no harm by what was said thoughtlessly. A little boy distressed his mother by killing butterflies. She had, without realizing the implication, herself stamped on slugs that were eating the young plants in her garden. The small boy had seen her action and killed likewise, without grasping the special grown-up motive of his mother. To kill any living creature in front of a child is to teach him how to become destructive.

A grandmother, who had just given up her own home in order to care for her motherless grandchildren and to start bringing up a family for the second time, said: "I had such a wonderful grandmother, I shall never forget her. How could I do less than be a good grandmother myself?" The example from her first years was still inspiring her so long afterwards. We owe as grown-ups more than we can count to what was done for us in early childhood. The mother who comforted us in our first troubles has taught us how to give comfort to those we meet in distress. The father who was big and strong enough to carry the child with weary legs has shown us how to help those, whose burdens are greater than ours. The person we saw remaining quiet when he might have been angry, being angry at wrong done to others, when he might have kept quiet, being brave when he might have pitied himself, being honest when he might have cheated, has written virtues into our childish hearts for our use in later years. When we look back to childhood, we can compose a long list of those to whom we are now grateful for the impressions they gave, for the examples they set. We can be glad of the childish talent for imitation which made us absorb into ourselves so much good.

As the child grows old enough for thought, some discussions about right and wrong will arise from time to time. Imitation will even then be more effective than explanation, which does not really convince the very young. Even at the age when a child asks a stream of questions starting with the word "why", he is in fact more interested in how things are in the world than their reason for being there. The "whys and wherefores" belong to a later stage of development. Pictures, which he can imagine, are more comprehensible to him than explanatory thoughts. When a piece of fine brave behaviour is described to him, he will exclaim: "I will do that too". If some wrongdoing is described, he may say: "O no, I will never do that". In such quiet moments, as for instance at bedtime, he can learn to recognize something of his own behaviour, if he is shown pictures of what he has done or he might do. If a bad habit needs to be broken like running into the forbidden street alone, he can be told the story of another little boy, who came to grief at doing just this. He will realize that the story imitates his own behaviour and will be far more impressed than if he is continually told that he is forbidden to run from the house. The cautionary tale, if it is childlike enough, has a real function. On the other hand the story of the good example will be equally effective, much more than the unfortunate custom of pointing to another child and saying: she is such a good girl, why can't you be like her? Far more attractive is the glamorous heroine, too good to be true, of a thrilling tale of good behaviour. "I want to be as good and beautiful as that" comes the echo.

How far should parents and grown-ups consider the needs of the children and when should children accept the wishes and wants of those who care for them? When the subject of upbringing is discussed, it can soon sound as if the grown-ups could have no life of their own for many years if they must constantly ask what is bad for the youngsters. In any family in which the children realize that they are the centre of everything, they can become selfish and demanding. Where there is more than one child the stages of development may well be different and the varying needs will have to be balanced one against the other. It is a natural part of moral experience in childhood to learn to fit into the community and it does no harm to the youngest of the family, for instance, if he hears and sees what is beyond his grasp, for the sake of the older ones. It is a fairly common sight in a museum or picture gallery to see little children, who can neither see nor appreciate the exhibits but who are there because the grown-ups or older brothers and sisters are interested. The little ones have usually found their own way of adapting themselves to the situation

38

such as enjoying the fun of running up and down the wide tracts of polished floor. It is quite a different matter when the grown-ups give way to the longing for a bit of indulgence, whether it means letting themselves go emotionally in front of the children or going off on a spree and bringing the whole family home far too late. Such things bring their own consequences, since the smallest infants are the most apt at reflecting back to those who bring them up their own behaviour.

If parents and grown-ups set the standard of right and wrong for the children, from whence shall they take it for themselves in the first place? There is no doubt that the task of bringing up babies into childhood and youth tests the religious and spiritual character of the parents, especially in the first years, when little help from outside the family can be expected. This period is also the most impressionable from the child's point of view, since experience goes so deeply into his nature by the force of imitation. It is most important that parents should give thought to what they are aiming at in their behaviour towards these human beings, whose early lives are entrusted to them. Natural instinct and a happy knack with little ones help when it comes to caring for them and playing with them. The deeper responsibilities of upbringing require a higher, more thoughtful sense of purpose, or, in one word, faith. They need faith in God and in the divine purpose of Man.

Can it be expected of parents that simply by having children they acquire much-needed faith if they did not know it already? Children are all born into a dilemma. The physical processes of birth are provided by Nature and the baby knows instinctively how to make his demands felt for physical care. But next to nothing is provided for the spiritual process of upbringing. The youngster expresses his needs but they can easily pass unheeded or be misunderstood. The consequence is then a soul deprived and misgrown, a young person at odds with himself and the world around him. Children are often expected to take their parents as they find them but fathers and mothers have to ask very much of themselves spiritually, if that which is needed is to be found. "We somehow trust" is an expression once used to describe faith, which might content a grown-up but never a child. He confronts the older people with a question that is asked unconsciously by his whole being. What kind of person do you wish me to become? I know how God made me in the world where I have been before I was born, what shall become of me in your world? What is God's idea of Man? Older people may have settled down to another or quite external picture of human existence on earth. The new-comer asks the biggest, highest question. What is God's idea? How can I behave accordingly?

The child brings goodness with him but he will learn here about wickedness of all kinds. Parents and grown-ups are not required to make him good but to help him to protect his goodness and adjust it to the conditions of life here on earth. They show him how to distinguish good from bad, how to follow the one and reject the other, for Man in the sight of God is intended to serve the Good. Thomas Traherne, the seventeenth-century poet with a genius for describing childhood, expresses the wonder of the soul who realizes how divinely he is intended to live on earth.

> "Am I a glorious Spring
>   Of joys and riches to my King?
> Are men made Gods? And may they see
>   So wonderful a thing
>   As God in me.
> And is my soul a mirror that must shine
> E'en like the sun and be far more divine?"

V

CELEBRATING FESTIVALS

THE first great festival in the life of the child is his reception here on the earth by the community into which he is born. His parents give him a family, a name, citizenship and a place in the world. But the part of him that does not depend on what the family gives, his individual self, comes into the world as a being in his own right, finding a relation to the community of Mankind. The greatness of this event has been at all ages in history expressed in religious ceremonies. Herein lies the origin of baptism in Christian churches of all denominations and of rites in other religions celebrated at the beginning of a child's life on earth. The birth into the family follows the course of Nature and the birth into Mankind is acknowledged in a religious manner. The eternal soul of the child has come from God and is received into the community of human beings, who recognize their common divine origin and the higher spiritual purpose to which they would dedicate themselves on earth. He comes to join them and is welcomed as a gift from the Divine World to the earthly world.

Doctrines explaining the religious significance of birth are varied from religion to religion, from church to church. Some stress the entry of the child into the family and the race, others the reception into a distinct Church, of which the newborn child becomes a member with obligations at the very start of his existence. It is not necessary to distinguish all these variations here, but more important to point out the common essence of all birth rites. Much confusion of thought is encountered in religious matters nowadays because the idea of religion has become so entangled with that of institutions that they are difficult to separate. Institutions are arrangements of society, religion is the need of a human being to find the right relation to the Divine in all aspects of his life. There is a great necessity for religious revival in this sense today. Thinking has become too limited and superficial, so that the questions of life are not asked in their essentials. People are much more apt to say: What is your religion, what does your family belong to, where is your place of worship? than to ask: what is the meaning of faith? how do we know God? what is the rightness of all the different religions in the world? A new way of thinking is needed, bold and universal, able to face the large realities of existence. How much this need is felt can be seen from the emergence in our times of universal thinkers, pioneers of ideas, whose example stirs us to enlarge and deepen our own thinking. The foremost of these is Rudolf Steiner, whose understanding of the whole cycle of human existence enables our thought to grasp the significance of religion as such. Once we have dared to ask how Man is related to God, it becomes possible to understand the value of each known religion and to see the special place in human history occupied by Christianity.

Such universal thinking is of the greatest worth in facing the practical problem of how religion should be placed into the life of the child. It is not enough to say, he belongs to the creed or denomination of his family and will be taken to places of worship with his relatives when he is old enough not to make a disturbance. Certainly such a procedure is in order and parents should decide what amount of public worship is required in the family. But the religious needs of the child are daily and continuous. They have to be met at home in the first years more than in public. They have little to do with creed and custom and very much with the understanding of the highest and most spiritual realities of human life. It is because universal thinking has to be re-discovered today that the upbringing of children presents us with so many problems of great interest.

The child is placed into the human religious community on earth by the ceremony or rites performed for him at the opening of his life. His parents or other responsible people will choose to which religious body he will be taken for this purpose. After he has been publicly received and acknowledged in this manner, his religious life will be lived for some years mostly at home. Besides the daily business of prayer and moral training, which has been already described, there are also the special festivals to be considered, that arise by custom from time to time. The seasons of the year bring most of them about as they change and move through its course. A valuable element is brought into family life when they are celebrated at home. Some customs will now be described, which are simple enough to follow in the house but which bring to the household experiences of great significance. They are not only suitable for small children. There will be no reason to stop them as the family grows up. They can well be cherished customs for many generations. The reason for including them at this point is the fact that they belong to the sphere of home, where the strong impressions are received in the early years. Just those little children who have taken part in these customs are the most likely to perceive their value and to insist on continuing them later.

Taken in order as the seasons of the year revolve, the first festival to be celebrated will be at the oncoming of winter. Christmas falls at midwinter and should according to old tradition be prepared during the four weeks that go before. In Christian terminology this period has the name of Advent. In the southern hemisphere Christmas comes at midsummer and the time of preparation is early summer. The religious festivals that have been established by old human custom correspond in the northern hemisphere with the rhythm of Nature through the course of the year and in the south are in contrast to the prevailing season. The celebration of the festivals may be the same but the experience will be different. In Adventtime there is a custom of lighting candles in the house, especially in the evening. It is one thing to light candles in the winter and quite another in the summer. In the southern continents the inner meaning of the candle as a symbol will appear more strongly than in the north, where the darkness of winter makes a natural background to the lighted rooms of the house. The candle signifies the flame of the human spirit burning in the human body. The candle flame gives off light and warmth as it consumes the wax and the wick. So the human spirit consumes the vitality of the body as it illumines and warms the world around.

It is of the greatest importance that real wax candles should be used. Electric lights are good decoration but poor symbols. No risk is run of setting the house on fire, if the candles are not left burning in an empty room. There can be no other experience showing to our hearts what it means for light to shine in darkness to be compared with watching a lighted candle in a dark place. What a large circle of light is thrown by even a small candle! How the colour of the light changes as it spreads into the darkness! How the shadows press against the outer rim of the circle that moves with the flickering of the flame. What power of warmth is spread from the small candle. How much the mind can think and see while the eyes are drawn in fascination to the flame. A candle is one of the earthly things transparent for spiritual experience.

Another Advent custom is to make a wreath of evergreen in token of the whole cycle of the year and to put four candles on it. The wreath is then hung with red ribbon and one of the candles is lighted for each Sunday before Christmas. It is again of great importance to make the wreath of living branches, of fir where that is available or other evergreen. Artificial imitations are not good symbols, which is true likewise of the Christmas tree. It should be a living tree that has grown in the earth and is capable of living and dying. Plants and trees grow from small seeds, take on visible shape stage by stage, then fade away into the invisible. They come and go between the visible world and the realm of the invisible, of the living world-ideas in the universe. Artificial flowers that become dusty but do not fade have no spiritual secrets to tell the soul.

The living Christmas tree has much to say. It is naturally dark and unadorned except with its many needles. It stands for the tree of the knowledge of Good and Evil, that from which the forbidden apple was eaten. This tree brought death into the world, as the effect of Man's fall. Before Christmas it is an old tradition to remember the story of Adam and Eve. The tree can be brought early into the house and hung with apples as a sign of the Fall. On Christmas Eve a wonderful transformation should be made. The apples should disappear or, if they are still fit, be turned into candlesticks by having holes made in the top. The tree should be decorated and covered with candles. The most meaningful decorations are stars, angels and the old signs for the seven planets. They can be made of metal, wood or gold paper.

44

The transparent tree is dark and flowerless no longer. It blossoms with the signs of the stars, and the flames of light. The angels look down from its branches, only paper-made symbols, it is true, but sharing visibly the invisible grace from the Heavens inspiring what is often called "the Christmas spirit". Nature has not given the tree its blossoms, but the human hands of people have done so, giving expression to the inner light flowering in the human soul. The darkness brought into Man's nature by the Fall is illumined by the light of the human Spirit. So the tree of the Fall, of death, is transformed into the Tree of Life, when the candles are lighted on Christmas Eve. If gifts are laid around it and distributed to those present they take on an inner value greater than their outer worth. They shine with the glow of true giving and receiving, the goodwill streaming from one heart to another.

The pattern of all givers at Christmastide is God Himself. Traditional customs express it in a variety of ways. The symbols of Christmas are stars, angel figures and lighted candles, representing, all of them, the world of the Heavens above. Singing has a special place in the affairs of this season, old carols being available in quantities that no other festival has inspired. When people sing they lift up their voices to a use beyond the daily one of talking and telephoning. One carol says: "O hush your noise, ye men of strife, and hear the angels sing," and, one might add, sing yourselves because singing will bring you nearer to the company of Heaven. People do not sing when their hearts are full of strife and anger, but when they feel joyful trust in the divine powers. Some say that the Christ-Child enters the house at Christmastime. Others show the children how to hang up empty stockings before they sleep on Christmas Eve and to look for them again in the morning when they will be full. Father Christmas has filled them and who is he but a picture for the Father in the Heavens who sends us the mysterious gift of Christmas? Such customs bring Heaven right down to earth at this season of the Holy Nights.

The Christmas festival has two parts. First come the twelve Holy Nights and then on January 6th Epiphany, or the coming of the Three Kings. Long ago the distinction was well observed but in modern times is largely forgotten. Those people who like to have a Christmas crib in the house can easily mark the change.

On Christmas Eve the figures of the scene of Bethlehem can be laid out, Mary, Joseph, the Child and the Shepherds coming with dogs and sheep. On January 6th the shepherds can be exchanged for the three Kings arriving with their gifts, gold, frankincense and myrrh, and a star can be put over the little house. Those who like to act plays with amateur players at home have the opportunity for three dramatic scenes at this season. In Advent the story of Adam and Eve in the garden of Paradise and the intrusion of the serpent can be acted. At Christmas the story of Bethlehem with the announcement of the angels to the shepherds can be made into a play in which the children can take part and at Epiphany that of the Kings can be treated in the same style. Many old legends are still known, connected with the event of Christmas, which can be turned into beautiful short plays well adapted to performances at home.

After winter comes the spring. It is a lovely thing for children to welcome the first buds and blossoms. Once upon a time divine blessing was called down on every event in Nature. The house, the plants, the cattle, the fields, all were blest. There survives from Celtic times a blessing for the seeds and another for reaping the harvest. The seeds to be sown in the garden can be heaped together and one of the old forms of blessing said. A song can be sung, which mentions all living creatures above and below, like that of St Francis, then the family can go out to sow the seeds. All festivals come about when the ordinary things of life are given their true spiritual significance, expressed in words and actions. Then human doings acquire proper dignity. In some families special customs may be invested spontaneously.

Spring brings in the northern hemisphere the preparation for Easter. Lent is in contrast to the joyful upsurging of Nature at this time. While the plants grow and sprout, another mood rises in the souls of people who understand the meaning of Easter. In Advent the Fall of Man is remembered before the coming of the Light into the darkness at Christmas. In Lent the consequences of the Fall are felt, the weakness in human nature, the fear of the Light, the temptation to reject, to betray and to deny. When people become conscious of the infection of Evil in themselves they look for a medicine against it. So it was that the custom arose of fasting in Lent which in its modern version usually means giving up a pleasant habit like eating sweets or smoking. But the old custom needs changing into another form. It is a far greater discipline today to do something that we are not obliged to do than to give something up. We are so beset with chores and duties, that we have difficulty in undertaking some good deed or spiritual study to which we are not obliged and which brings no other reward than itself. The good in us is strengthened and refreshed by such free actions, which are of more spiritual benefit than a quantity of repentance. Very few people feel that they are inwardly, or in behaviour, all that they would wish to be. Without wishing to be called miserable sinners, they would like to be cured of much weakness and to grow in rightful self-respect. The readiest means to this end is to arrange with one's self to study a serious book, start a course of meditation, or specially help someone in need. The soul grows in goodness and trust. Naturally, young children will not be able to enter into such grown-up considerations. But they will receive a deep impression if they observe the Lenten attitude in the older people around them. In their own way, they will be able to join in, by undertaking a regular kind action towards someone nearby or trying of their own will to develop a new good habit in their own affairs. Such efforts need not stop with Lent but they can very well be started then, in awareness of what the season brings home to us about ourselves.

Good Friday has a remarkable atmosphere, which persists whether people observe it in their behaviour or not. An awed hush comes over the creatures of Nature noticeable to everyone who has the heart to feel it. The birds sing a more sober song, the flowers are quietly watchful, the trees seem to listen. Even if the weather is bright, the brightness is softened beyond the usual. It seems a barbarous thing to treat it as an ordinary working day on the one hand, or on the other to make it an occasion for parties and outings. It should be a quietly serious day for people as it is for plants and birds. The mystery of Easter is well beyond the scope of mind in young children but not beyond the wisdom of the heart to recognize a solemn festival of remembrance. Christmas has brought the clear joy of the Light shining with us here on earth. Holy Week brings the solemn sadness over the failure of Mankind to protect the Light from being attacked by the darkness. Every right-minded child can feel this fact even if he cannot comprehend it and is grateful for being allowed a quiet and solemn day on Good Friday.

Easter Day is full of a stronger, deeper joy. We celebrate then the victory of the Light over the darkness, of Life won back from death. Without the solemn mood that went before, the joy of Easter would not reach full strength. The birds sing of it, the flowers glow with it, and people feel in their hearts the new-born life of the Spirit. They long to make their life on earth more full of goodness, more devoted to the Spirit, more worthy in purpose. The divine Light has not refused the attack of the darkness but has accepted suffering and the descent into death. Now on Easter morning the Light has risen again, overcoming the stifling power of darkness, mastering the annihilating strength of death. Man's existence is not to be swallowed up by Evil but is to evolve in the power of the divine Light towards the Transfiguration. The children should share the solemn joy of Easter. The little ones can grasp its meaning best in the living parable offered by Nature in the form of the butterfly. They should be shown, not once but each year, the fat caterpillars and the delicate butterflies and told how the one changes into the other by a process of death within the shrine of the cocoon. The butterfly, the creature of light, emerges triumphant from the darkness. His life-story is the best lesson in the meaning of Easter.

The best-known custom marking this festival is the search for the magic eggs. They are prepared by a variety of methods. They can be hard-boiled hens' eggs dyed in bright colours or painted in patterns as decorative as the skill of the grown-ups allows. They can be empty eggshells similarly decorated or filled with chocolate. They can be chocolates or marzipan eggs. Where circumstances allow, they should be hidden out of doors in a garden and the children should hunt for them. The egg is a clear symbol of new life but at Easter the eggs are not ordinary but magic. They are brightly coloured and they are hidden by a magical being who always just escapes being seen, the Easter hare. He may leave a chocolate figure of himself behind along with edible chickens and ducklings. But he is invisible because he belongs to the Moon and brings eggs which no hare on earth can do. He is a being from a very old tradition about the fertility of Nature in Springtime inspired by the influence of sun and moon on the earth.

Ascension and Whitsuntide are festivals which continue and conclude the cycle of Easter. An adult mind is required to set about grasping their meaning but the children should be made aware of them in pictures. At Ascension we remember how the Light who came down at Christmas and overcame the darkness at Easter, unites again with the light in the Heavens of sun, moon and stars. In their light live the angels and archangels and all the company of Heaven, who celebrate Ascension with us. Nature shows its picture of the festival in the flowering of the trees. They are transfigured by their blossoms at this season, while they are green and earthy at all other times of year. A special excursion is a suitable celebration within the family, perhaps to a botanical garden, or to some place where the beauty of the world is particularly to be appreciated. Whitsuntide is, in contrast, connected with that which is at work within the soul of Man. Wisdom about the soul is learnt by children from animals, who show its qualities each in their own particular way. The Whitsun outing can be taken to a zoological garden or to a farm where domestic animals are kept. The children should learn to see what the human being has in common with the animals and what he has for himself, though which he can attain to control over the animal nature. Their hearts can begin to feel how the divine Spirit lives as light within the human soul.

Midsummer is the opposite in the course of the year to Christmas and is connected in Christian custom with St John the Baptist. The sun is at its height, the days at their longest, the nights at their shortest. By old tradition this festival should be celebrated with a bonfire out of doors at night under the stars. When the strength of the sun is about to start declining, people on earth show their light to the beings who look down through the light of the stars in the burning fire with upward streaming flames. A certain moral element is contained in this symbol. The fire is a token of purification and as it dies down the people present should jump over it to express the burning away of human impurity. Children easily understand this, if they are told to burn away their grumbles and bad temper. At the kindling of the fire a speech should be made, not to explain but to express its moral significance. This should be followed by singing and country dancing, for these are the two arts that belong to midsummer. Although the custom of lighting fires is older than Christianity, all that John the Baptist stands for is in harmony with the older meaning of the festival. He was the herald of Christ's coming and the awakener of the conscience through his preaching and his baptism in the people of his time. He proclaimed the indwelling power of the divine Light, which shines within us in our sensitivity to right and wrong. It is good in the summer months of the year to remember him and the other great saints and heroes of the past, in whom the Light shone brightly. Their lives will supply many fine stories for the children.

With the coming of autumn in the northern hemisphere and spring in the southern, the festival of Michaelmas arrives. It is named after the archangel Michael, who by old tradition is our defender against the power of Evil, the dragon. In the north this is harvest-time. Michael was thought of old to be the archangel of death who harvests the good and bad in human souls. His festival can be partly a celebration of the fruits of the earth, corn, fruit and flowers being assembled for this purpose. A grace can then be said, blessing the food of the whole year. Michaelmas gives a special opportunity for drama, provided by the many legends of the prowess of the Archangel or his human counterpart St George against the Devil. Home-made plays for children and grown-ups are most easily fashioned out of legends. Decorations for Michaelmas can be made by binding the stalks of straw together in the shape of five-pointed stars. They can be hung up until winter comes, when they can become a contribution of Michaelmas to Christmas. Lanterns belong to this season, when we celebrate the inner power of the divine Light in the soul to bring forth courage and brave deeds. In a lantern we see light shining from within a frame as the spiritual light shines from within our bodies. Many kinds can be made at home, with materials like paper and glass jars, or even from turnips and pumpkins suitably hollowed out. A lantern procession at dusk makes very significant to children the meaning of the light that shines within.

Celebrating festivals illumines our life on earth with heavenly meaning and shows us the significance of our human existence in the universe. We human beings stand between the two worlds uniting them in ourselves. We are the crossing point where the upper circle representing the Heavens flows into the lower one belonging to the earth. We feel and show the children how to feel towards the divine Universe as Thomas Traherne thought when he wrote these lines:

> "That all things should be mine
> This makes His bounty most divine
> But that they all more rich should be,
> And far more brightly shine,
> As used by me;
> It ravishes my soul to see the end
> To which this work so wonderful doth tend."

Part Two

Childhood

I

THE CHILD'S NEED FOR GOD

THE child's main occupation is growing. His limbs lengthen, his capacities develop, his experience increases. He is continually changing and learning, discarding and acquiring. His soul lives altogether in the mood of becoming, which was once experienced by a nine-year-old who said one morning: "I am quite different today. I shall never be the same again." The grown-ups require to make an effort of mind if they are to be in proper sympathy with the growing child. They need to recall their own experiences of childhood vividly, to recapture for instance the shock on the threshold of adult life of the discovery that clothes are no longer grown out of or have to be let down. They just wear out or become old-fashioned. The shock of such a moment is useful as a signpost to the earlier stages of childhood and adolescence when the body was continually presenting surprises and changes. Imagination is required on the part of the grown-ups to keep pace with the child's experience of constant change. The world seems to him to be going through frequent revolutions, as his mental and emotional capacities develop and he realizes much that he previously passed by or pushed away. The adult view of the world is often far too fixed and settled, and therefore out of tune with what is actually taking place. The child's experience sees the changing face of things almost out of proportion and only active imagination can bridge the gap.

A major crisis in growth is signalled in the child's life by the loss of the first teeth at about six years old. Up to that time he has been involved mainly in developing, since he was born, the powers of the body and the capacity to walk, speak and think. He has lived in the shelter of life at home with glimpses of the world beyond to prepare him for the moment when he has to step out on his own. For the most part he will be doing this for the first time when he starts school. There are, of course, children whose upbringing does not follow this pattern, whose homes are not places of shelter or who lose them too early, who are exposed to the world of school or institution before the proper stage in growth. Their development will be different and unless they have exceptional strength of character, they will be liable to carry many weaknesses into their later years. If the healthy pattern is followed, the child will leave infancy behind when his teeth change at about six years old and will step out into childhood, strong in the forces gathered in his early years. His body will then be so far grown that he can enter on a new stage in which the forces of his mind can expand freely. The body will continue to change but its development will no longer be the full-time occupation that it has been. The child will be able to begin developing much more strongly the forces of the soul. He will be hungry for experience of people and of the world, which his home cannot provide. He will be ready to step out into the wider community of the school.

Growing-up brings many thrills with it, suddenly being able to do something out of reach a short time ago, feeling the limbs stronger, the understanding wider. Children have an eager interest in the things they cannot yet do, in the people who are bigger and cleverer than they are. They look constantly forward, experimenting and aiming at something new. They are thrilled with themselves and with life. But there is another side to the picture equally real. That is the threat of fear. Just as much as the thrill, children feel the fears of life. Supposing we cannot do it, supposing we fall and are hurt, supposing someone is angry with us and many more such threats to the cheerful way of things are felt. Growing-up is double-sided, bringing pleasure and pain, joy and fear, and the contending with failure as much as achievement. In the first years the light shone from behind and the darkness was in front but in the following period of childhood the way at every step lies through the interplay of light with darkness. The soul is in constant tension between longing and dread, wanting to hold to the light but struggling with the darkness.

For the process by which the child becomes a man we use the expression "growing-up" which well describes what takes place physically. From a small and helpless creature, he grows into a large and capable person as far as the body is concerned. From a spiritual point of view, however, the expression should in reality be changed into "growing-down". The spiritual being of the child has to make its way down from the worlds of Light, the dwelling-place before birth, into existence on earth. His spirit has to learn another way of living in other surroundings, where spiritual realities are exchanged for material ones. It is an experience of descent from Light into darkness, from divine protection into the hazards of life as we know it here. In a picture taken from the teaching recorded in the Gospels, the descent is called "the journey into the far country". It is going abroad in the biggest sense of the word. All that we go through in adult life when starting on foreign travel is a faint likeness to the experience we cannot really remember of leaving one world for another at birth. There is the wrench of leaving home, the shelter and the familiar conditions. The decision to depart has been made but when it comes to the point, there is the temptation to draw back. The plans have been decided upon, the route mapped out, but the preparations may prove inadequate, and the journey too strenuous and difficult. The last hesitation is overcome, the plunge taken, but the luggage has to be taken care of, lest part of the outfit of forces for soul and body should be lost. The unknown opens ahead. The conditions are new and untried. The language of thought and viewpoint has to be learnt. The new people to be met are strange and slow to understand the traveller's needs. The climate, the way of living, the experiences are all so different, so hard to get used to, so interesting but presenting fresh problems at every turn. And this great venture abroad, this biggest journey of existence, has to be undertaken in the most helpless condition of mind and body that we can know, the child's. Growing down to earthly life is the biggest most thrilling adventure but fraught with the greatest risks and fears.

There was once a small child whose earliest experience of the world was a garden. There was grass to run about on, a bank to roll down, steps to climb and jump. Paths ran between flower-beds down to vegetable plots and the fruit trees. In the first years the child was very happy among the flowers. Grown-up people seemed so tall, their heads so far off. Dogs and horses were attractive but big and liable to turn fierce. But the snapdragons and nasturtiums were always friendly and the right size for companionship to the one who ran up and down the paths. But just in the middle of the garden was a little glasshouse, a mysterious place full of pots and tools, and appearing from a damp, dark corner would come a large speckled toad, ancient, wrinkled-looking and ominous. Outside was the child's garden of Paradise, but inside was the toad, a threat of lurking evil. It made no difference that older and braver children liked the toad and that she once produced a row of miniature offspring. That child saw the world in the first years as a meaningful picture on the same pattern as that described at the beginning of the Bible in the book of Genesis. Among the flowers was Paradise but interwoven with the first memories there was the hidden threat, the toad standing in for the serpent.

As that same small child grew older and bigger the world beyond the garden opened out before the mind that would now grasp a wider range of experience. Where the little town ended the walls lined with trees began, which enclosed the fields. At intervals the walls were broken by five-barred gates. One day the child, who was just entering on the second epoch of child-hood, put a head between the bars and saw on the far side of one of the gates a slope of green pasture falling away and beyond a line of rounded hills, the green broken here and there with patches of ploughed land and clumps of trees making strange shapes on their sides. The child had been born among these hills but had never consciously seen them before. The grown-ups, who knew the view by heart, did not realize what a revolution was taking place in the child's soul, for whom a great gate of life was opening at that moment. Distances began to be real, the green landscape spread itself out, the blue sky with the white ships of the clouds sailing over it came into view overhead. The wide world of earth and sky revealed itself to the child's mind that had become capable of seeing and knowing it in one flash of consciousness. Outwardly it was an afternoon like others and the walk proceeded as before. The child can recall this event in grown-up years but would have been quite incapable of speaking about what had happened at the time. Children can go through the greatest revolutions of development and be completely unable to give a sign to those around them.

Something also happened, however, in those days. Other children came on those walks and games were often played. One was called "animal, vegetable, mineral". Someone present would think of something under one of these headings, while the others tried to guess what it was, but at the offset they had to know to which class it belonged. One who wished to tease the others chose a person, though human beings were not included in the game. Protests followed from the other children but the aunt in charge announced firmly that men and women were after all animals of a higher kind. The particular child who had previously discovered through the bars of the gate the beauty of the wide world, looked out over the sunny hills which they could all see in their walk, and saw the light darken. A black cloud of fear rose from the childish heart and seemed to blot out the sun. An inner voice cried: it is not true, it cannot be true but it has been said. There was no arguing with the aunt, the grown-ups knew and yet it seemed as if a great untruth had been spoken before God and Man. The serpent had spoken in Paradise, and the wonder of the world began to withdraw. That child without realizing that experience was, as it were, quoting the Bible, heard in the depths of the heart the gates begin to close that shut behind Adam and Eve when they were driven out from the garden, where the Lord walked in the cool of the evening.

There is much to see, to learn and to do in the world outside the gate of Paradise. After the first shock, the soul adjusts itself to a new existence. The child begins to accept the experience that for all laughter there are tears, that joy can follow sorrow, and sorrow joy. Failure is mixed with achievement, ugliness with beauty, truth with untruth. As the world around him grows different, the child becomes with every shock of experience, happy or unhappy, more aware of himself. His spiritual being enters further into the house of the body and he becomes capable of loneliness. The essence of growing-up is the experience of loneliness, of something which in itself is one of the great contradictions of our life on earth. In one sense it is pain, in another the triumph of the self, without which the personality cannot mature. The growing child must be allowed to enter into it and be saved from the continual distractions to which children are often exposed today. Plenty happens to a child every day of childhood but he needs the opportunity to realize that in his own being he is alone. He even needs periods of outer quiet from time to time, so that he can occasionally turn back into himself. There is, of course, a wrong kind of loneliness that can harm a child who is neglected or an older person who has too little connection with other people. Self-centredness brings with it the misery of the child who will not play with others or the grown-up who feels unwanted. But true loneliness is essential to the development of inwardness to become capable of which is the need of every growing child.

The mystery of loneliness is the source of religious feeling. We are lonely first and foremost here on earth because we are separated from the Divine World, from our original existence in God. Being born is the first step in separation, but the soul is still accompanied in the first years by living memories and connections with the World from which he has come. As the process of growing-up continues and the experiences of this earthly world increase, the soul becomes more aware of the separation and more capable of loneliness. Childhood memories of one person may have been described but the pattern of experience within them is common to all children. Most grown-ups, looking back, will be able to recognize that in other settings and conditions, they passed through the process of awakening to this world as if they were being driven out of the garden of Paradise. The Bible describes in forceful pictures the facts of existence that are encountered by us all through being born and growing-up. Because we have been driven out, we can be lonely. All lesser kinds of loneliness that can be felt are details in the original, cosmic loneliness from the Divine World, which is the essence of our existence on earth. The word religion comes from a Latin root meaning "to bind back". We look back to God, we feel the need to pray, we attempt to make a new contact with the Divine because we are cut off and are lonely. The religious need of the small child is to live in the memory of his life before birth, but the older one is ready to look for the new religion that is found in the life here on earth. His first step will be to find loneliness.

Selfhood is the outcome of the great separation from the world in which he lived before birth. In the Bible story of Adam and Eve, it is said that after the eating of the forbidden fruit, the man and the woman became self-conscious, recognizing their nakedness. Every child goes through many stages in becoming conscious of himself, as he realizes the distinction between self, other people and the world. At each stage he feels his nakedness in a new way, not as a physical experience but as a psychological one. Many childish fears and much shyness come from this cause. But there is no going back on the way of becoming a grown-up and selfhood is the essential element in a fully developed human being on earth. In the pain of feeling lonely, the sense of selfhood awakens. In the pain of losing the nearness of the Divine World, it ripens. Can something now be found for what is being left behind? Is there gain to be discovered in the loss? From such an inner question the religious longing of the growing child arises. A poetic expression for the trouble of childhood is found at its best in the poetry of Wordsworth, a poet of the nineteenth century.

> "But there's a Tree, of many one,
> A single field which I have looked upon,
> Both of them speak of something that is gone:
> The Pansy at my feet
> Doth the same tale repeat.
> Whither is fled the visionary gleam?
> Where is it now, the glory and the dream?"

The need of the child's soul, when the natural nearness of God s withdrawn, is to find a new relation to Him here in this other kind of existence on earth. He will tend to look in three ways for the religious experience he needs. The world of earth is not impregnated with the Divine Presence as is the world of Heaven. But the earth was created at the beginning of time by God and bears the impress of His creation. The child will look to the beauty of earth, sea and sky, and to the wisdom in the life of bird, fish and beast to find the Being of God in His works. He will wish to grow in reverence for all that is beautiful in the world. He will be eager to see and know more of the ways that stones, plants and animals exist each after their own kind. But he will crave for the working of the Divine to be revealed to him in all such experiences. If he can feel the warmth and brightness in the sun's beams to be a revelation of the love of God in the Heavens for His creatures on earth he will be satisfied. He will see the flowers opening upwards to the sun and feel them giving thanks for the light. Birds in flight, fish gliding, animals running and leaping will be using in joy the powers that God has given. The quiet hills and still rocks will seem to manifest the upholding patience of God. Those who bring him up or educate him can very easily frustrate his search for the divine forces revealed in Nature. They may have too little reverence in their hearts to recognize sufficiently the wonder of what is beautiful and wise in the world. If they are to help the child, they will need to know what it is to worship God in the greatness of their wonder, and to show him how to worship also.

The second religious experience sought by the growing soul of the child comes with realizing the divine meaning in life on the earth. He feels throughout his being the impulse to grow up, which gives him his natural energy and determination to live. But he looks into the world to learn from those who have been here longer the value of life. He looks to see the working of God in human beings, in what they do and say, in what happens to them. Children can be very inquisitive in their search for God. They will be deprived of the religious experience they need if the older people cannot show them how God works in themselves and in their lives. Unbelieving, cynical people, go-getters out for what they can make, weak compromisers suffering all, hinder the children who are looking for the signs of God in those whom they meet. At the time in life when the seed of faith should begin to germinate and to sprout the frost of disappointment settles on the young soul. But when on the other hand, the children encounter people with wise understanding and high ideals, when they can feel themselves warmed with real love by them, then divine light quickens the seed of faith. What blossom and fruit will be born in later years is beyond calculation.

The third religious experience, which the child needs, comes when he finds the presence of the Divine within himself. He begins to realize the strength in his limbs and the life in his body as he recognizes them also in other people and other creatures. But when he is quiet, and especially perhaps when he is alone, he feels the divine spirit thinking, living, moving within himself. He awakes to the precious treasure that belongs only to him, for which he should be responsible. He has already grown considerably in the knowledge of Good and Evil since his earthly life began. Goodness seems worthy of himself, wrong thoughts and actions make him feel degraded. He naturally feels that the will of God has brought him into life and should be expressed in his thoughts, words and deeds, but beyond all that he can recognize within himself, there lies something unknown in the distance of time. A mystery of the Spirit awaits him, for which he will be ready only when he is older. The sense lives dimly in his heart that a revelation greater than that which he knew before he was born is prepared for him here. He must keep himself awake and make himself worthy for what is to come. The child relies on those around him to share his belief in the future mystery and to prevent him from being hindered in his striving towards it. He feels himself to be on a quest and only the grown-ups can help him who share his conviction.

Certain pictures from the Bible, from the Old Testament, have been described to illustrate the spiritual experiences of the growing child. In the New Testament there is a parable told in the Gospel of St Matthew which can be understood in relation especially to the third experience of childhood. It opens with the saying that the Kingdom of Heaven is like ten maidens. In the picture language of the Bible the human soul as such is seen in human form. The maidens are young souls, not yet fully grown, waiting for the revelation of the Spirit, for the coming of the Bridegroom in the future, at an hour they cannot foresee. While they wait, they sleep, for the ordinary daily consciousness on earth is from a spiritual standpoint a sleep of the soul. Nevertheless they have to be prepared for what is to come. They all have lamps in their hands, but with a difference. Some have the oil ready for the lamps and will be able to light them at any time. Others wait until the bridegroom is announced before looking for the oil. Those who are ready beforehand go into the marriage, when the bridegroom comes. Those who have gone to look for oil return to find the door shut and are left outside. The religious education of the growing child means helping him to prepare his oil, so that his lamp can be lighted at the right hour. He will have to light it himself. Perhaps no one will be at hand to help him just then. But if the oil is ready and sufficient, he will be prepared to go forward to meet that for which he has waited. The religion of the child will be fulfilled in the spiritual life of the grown-up.

II

TEACHING RELIGION TO THE CHILD

As soon as the child is old enough to attend school, he should have instruction in religion as in other subjects. He has been learning religion since he was born while he has been learning about life, but at this period he begins to want knowledge imparted to him by way of instruction. Children whose development has not been forced too early, enjoy acquiring knowledge. Their growing minds are full of questions and if the lessons are well given, they come as welcome answers to the searching and inquiring. Throughout human life, the ability to learn depends on the inner activity of questioning, which comes naturally to the healthy child in early years. Like many other good gifts, it can be lost or wasted. If it is rightly cared for, the child should grow up into a person who seeks knowledge for himself, who can in mature years face with a free mind the biggest questions of existence, of life, death and eternity. The first consideration in teaching him should be the care and cultivation of his capacity for questioning. He will need encouragement to ask the right questions, that is to say those that are capable of receiving fruitful answers. Superficial ones, a series of unthinking "whys" are of no use to him. Neither will he benefit by receiving what seem to be complete answers, that settle the matter. He will need to be shown how to question further and more deeply, how to look beyond the horizon of what he knows to the greater spaces of the Unknown and how to venture on ahead. In this matter the art lies in finding the way between two extremes. To answer a question so that there is nothing left to ask is like banging the door of the mind shut against the immensity of the universe. On the other hand the child will lose his confidence in life if he does not receive a precise and straight answer. He will be stricken with fear, if he learns that there are many things we do not know and never can know. But it will satisfy him to hear that we have to grow in wisdom in order to understand the mysterious ways of God. He will accept the thought that we have to be both strong and worthy to receive fuller answers than those we know today. A child does not expect to know in the same way as a grown-up. He recognizes naturally that his mind is still in process of growing its wings. He wants the older people to be sure of themselves, but not content with their present limitations. Two attitudes which are really opposites both harm the child. The one says: we do not know, we cannot know, we are not meant to know. The other says: we know now today that it is like this and this and that is the last word on the subject.

It is especially important in the sphere of religion to safeguard the ability to search and question. A short time ago on the top of a London bus, two young men on their way to the business part of the City, were overheard discussing religion. One said to the other something like this: I was well brought up, my parents took me to Church and saw that I was properly taught. They provided me with a childhood faith and I am very grateful to them. I don't bother much about religion now, I have what they gave me. It was quite evident that the young man was not wearing his childhood clothes, nor living on the pocket money given to him as a boy. But in spiritual matters he was satisfied with a childhood faith which he expected to be sufficient for the rest of his life. In every other respect, he expected to grow up and develop but not in religion, where he was content to remain childish. Another danger arises, when faith is thought of as a natural part of childhood but unnecessary later on, something to be left behind, when entering the sober world of material realities. Where this point of view prevails, the age at which religion can be given up is getting earlier and earlier. Another young man was heard to say: My parents brought me up properly, I went to Sunday School, I heard the Bible stories and the hymns, and that is that. By the age of twelve he had been through it all. "And when I became a man, I put away childish things" wrote St Paul, but he meant that he changed his child's questions into those of the grown-up. He was not putting away religion as itself a childish thing. In all religious instruction the sense of adventure should be preserved and the child should learn to look forward to the time when he will be old and wise enough to search for himself beyond the limit of what he is taught. Then there is the hope that he will meet his parents and teachers again, not as those who bring him up, but as companions in the grown-up quest for the truth of God.

Who is to give instruction in religion? Three groups of people come in question, parents from the side of the family, teachers on behalf of the school, ministers representing the Church. On principle it could be said that all these groups are equally responsible. In practice the responsibility may come to rest more with one than the others. Their relation to the child in matters religious will be different and therefore all three are necessary. The parents lead the child into his life on earth, giving him the spiritual and material equipment he will need in order to be able to live from his own powers later. They should see that he has the means of faith and at no point in his upbringing should they feel able to give away their share of responsibility to other people, even to experts. Spiritual things cannot find their right place in the child's life if he does not observe their importance in the lives of his parents. His teachers inform him about the world and show him how to use and develop his abilities. But there is no part of life unrelated to religion. It is important for children, especially in the first half of schooling, to see all that they learn related to a whole. They should not learn here a bit of this and there a bit of that, without all being brought together in one. They should see the whole of life inspired by the working of God and their lessons as the means of knowing more and in greater detail about His universe. At one time it was considered impossible to have sound learning without true religion, a view that remains enshrined in the motto of the ancient university of Oxford. The task of teachers is to inspire all branches of learning with the reverence for the Divine. They may be of a variety of religious faiths and they need not teach their own beliefs in school. But the children need a religious outlook and feeling in every subject they learn.

The ministers give instruction on behalf of the Church or community in which the parents wish the children to be brought up. Sometimes considerations of nationality or tradition decide this matter and the personal faith of the parents may be on different lines. The whole matter of differing religions or separate denominations within the Christian Church may seem to produce nothing but confusion in modern times. But the fact remains that religion should have an expression in the life of the community apart from home and school. The child should be instructed in the beliefs of the religion chosen for him and sent to the ministers for that purpose. This may mean in practice going to Sunday School or following customs of quite a different kind.

Instruction is bound to depend very much on the beliefs of those who give it. But religion is in reality much more than a matter of doctrine. There is divine truth of universal proportions, which shines through the various religious forms known today. It is as much common to them all as the sun is the common light behind the many-coloured reflection cast from a window of stained glass. Because this is so, some main principles can be considered, which should operate in the instruction given to children, at different stages of childhood. Certain experiences are needed by the child as he grows and develops. By the time that he has come to school age, he is beginning to lose some of his natural unthinking sense for what is divine. The poet Wordsworth in his ode on "Intimations of Immortality from Recollections of Early Childhood" has expressed the sense of loss that comes with growing up.

> "There was a time when meadow, grove and stream,
>   The earth, and every common sight,
>   To me did seem
>   Apparelled in celestial light,
> The glory and the freshness of a dream.
> It is not now as it has been of yore,
>   Turn whereso'er I may,
>   By night or day,
> The things which I have seen I now can see no more."

Some gain must be found to take the place of this inevitable loss.

That which disappears in natural feeling can come back again in understanding. The child can begin to grasp with his mind how the creatures of Nature live and have their being under the guidance of divine wisdom. He will already know something about flowers and animals. Now he can grasp the wonder of the changes they pass through and make clear to himself what character of soul they each represent. He can see the effect they have upon each other and follow the drama which is continually being played out in every corner of the earth among the living creatures. Something he will learn by simply observing what goes on but this belongs more particularly to his lessons in Nature study. When he receives religious instruction, he should be made aware of the spiritual significance of what he has seen. He should perceive the details as parts within the whole universe, through which the mind of the Creator comes to expression. There are a number of ways of arriving at this experience. The life-story of an animal or an insect can prove a good means, as the grown-ups would agree, who have ever read any of the writings of the French naturalist, Fabre. Fables, like the ancient ones of Aesop, are another. The soul qualities of the animals are particularly described in such stories. Fairy tales, belonging entirely to the sphere of imagination, show in pictures the influences of soul at work in the creatures of Nature and in human beings. Many of these stories may be known to children before they are at school, but it is likely to have been in simplified versions or at least it will have been the simpler stories out of the great wealth that exists. Children learn most readily by means of the imagination throughout the first years of education.

Legends in great variety are available from the folklore of many nations today, when the treasures of literature are so widely known. They are mostly of great religious value, for they come from earlier periods of human history, when people were less inclined to divide the spiritual from the material than they are today. They were skilful in reading the working of divine wisdom in the created world. Old fairy stories and legends are in fact more often reliable than modern imitations. It is difficult nowadays to get sufficiently clear of the intellect and of sentiment for the eye of imagination to see distinctly how influences of soul work in the world independently of human personalities.

Stories should be avoided which describe the creatures of Nature behaving in a falsely human way. But if we look a long way back we find such stories, entirely true in the imaginative sphere, as those that Buddha told to his followers, about monkeys, swans, elephants, deer and many other creatures.

The art of instruction consists very much in bringing to the child the content he needs at the right moment. After his school life has begun, the time will come when he wants to go forward to a new stage and find out more about the working of God. All religions have their treasures of legends about the beginning of the world and man's early history. In a great variety of pictures, they speak of the same theme. In early times divine beings lived close to human beings, dwelling with them on earth, teaching them, inspiring them, leading them by the hand. Then the gods began to withdraw, less powerful ones could still appear from time to time, but the darkness began to fall between the realms of Heaven and Man's life on earth. In the Norse mythology, from which Wagner took the themes for some of his operas, the process is called "The Twilight of the Gods". In the Celtic legends different races of gods are described, who withdraw one after the other, until only the demi-gods, half-hero, half-god are left. In the world of the Greek gods, we watch how they gradually cease to dwell with men but how they retain for a long while the power to appear in hours of dilemma to take a guiding hand in human affairs. Stories such as these are called myths or legends, but they are nevertheless true accounts of history. It is a modern prejudice to reckon as historical only material events of which some written record can be traced. A child's sense of truth is wiser and will recognize that real spiritual events are described in the imaginative histories of gods and heroes.

Children should not be overloaded with too much material. They are glad to hear the same story again and again and to dwell for long periods in one world of pictures. There is no need to immerse them in the myths and legends of all nations. It is stimulating to discover a wealth of unknown mythology in later years, even after growing-up, when the mind has a wider range. What is important in childhood is to enter the world where history was once made between gods and men and to realize their parting from each other. If this is done through Norse stories, then the child's mind can usefully live with them for a long period, if the Celtic ones are chosen or the Greek, then they should be thoroughly explored. The deepening of experience is most important since the soul becomes confused and weak through too much distraction. At the period in his own life when the child is feeling how the protection of the Divine World, from which he came at birth, is being taken from him, he is ready to know how once this same experience befell Mankind in the past. He can realize imaginatively how he himself is part of the human race, how his child's question is a universal one: how does God work now in my life, since the divine forces have withdrawn from around me?

The first, earliest view of religion should be of something universal, common to all Mankind. In the ancient world, before the time when Christianity began, people were divided into races and tribes, each with their own religion. They were born into beliefs and customs in the same way as they were into family and citizenship. What was known about God at that stage of history was spread out through the peoples of the world, each being inspired with a particular aspect or understanding. All religions were true and in their own sense right. Christianity is the first universal religion in history. The Romans made an attempt to produce a universal element within the Empire by erecting a temple, the Pantheon in Rome, where statues of all the gods worshipped by the tribes under their rule were assembled. But the custom produced no inner reality, and remained only an outer form. The child's mind will be open to a true view of early religion, if he is introduced to the stories of the gods in the sense that they will show different aspects of the Divine World, as different peoples on earth could once understand them. He will then be prepared for the approach to the Bible, for an insight into its place in history and the special, universal quality of its inspiration.

In one sense the first half of the Bible, the Old Testament, speaks about the folk-religion of the Hebrew people, under the inspiration of their god, Jehovah. In another sense, it transcends the tribal limits and gives a picture of Man's beginning and his history of universal worth. The secret of this contradiction lies in the fact that the Hebrew people descending from Abraham had a mission in history different from that of the other peoples of the ancient world. They were a tribe it is true, but as one people they represented Mankind and mirrored its evolution in their experiences and doings. As they stood for Mankind, so their god Jehovah was the revelation of God Himself the Father of all peoples, who in the other gods could show only a portion of His being. Jehovah was stern with his tribe, reproving, punishing and commanding them because their special calling gave their behaviour great significance. There is no clearer picture in world-literature of Man's early relation to God than that to be found in the stories of the Old Testament. The child should learn them at the period in his life, when he is ready to explore the dealings of God with men. Many parents and teachers do not wait until children are seven, eight or nine years old to tell these stories. But if they are told too soon, they can come as a shock to the minds of the children and produce religious fears and doubts, which last on as prejudices into later life.

In the teaching of religion, the idea of Man's evolution is a necessity. Mankind has gone through different stages of development himself and can feel history repeated in his own experience. The grown-ups are liable to grasp this less easily and to need effort to realize that the stories of the Old Testament are true but that they reveal a past relationship between God and Man. A thread of meaning runs through what is told from the opening of the Book of Genesis to the last books of the prophets. First comes the story of the Creation of the World and of Man by God. Then follows the Fall of Man into sin and of the world into a place of labour and suffering. From that point onwards history becomes an ever-increasing dilemma. God leads His people, but they are not always obedient. Each step onwards is also a step downwards. The great men of the Old Testament are leaders, but they are also inventors of wickedness. The early Patriarchs were devoted to the Divine Will and could still on occasions talk with God. The later ones, beginning with Jacob, invented sin after sin, although Jehovah did not leave them unguided. Jacob discovered cheating, with great effect because those round him were too innocent to recognize deception. But his descendants were all able to learn guile and the stories become darker and darker. Jehovah gave to Moses the sacred Law written on tablets of stone, providing standards of behaviour to protect men against their own increasing wickedness. But the downward trend of evolution went on. At each stage men, even those chosen of God, were more and more cut off from His presence. The prophets appeared, messengers of His Will to warn and command. They did not speak out of themselves, they were mouthpieces of Jehovah, respected or attacked as their hearers welcomed or rejected their messages. In the midst of the growing world-dilemma, the souls of men were lightened and cheered by wonderful experiences of God's goodness and of His wisdom manifested in the sky, the earth and the hills, in all that lives and moves. The Psalms with their alternating patterns of light and shade, of peace and conflict, of joy and grief are a true picture of Man's life on earth in the time before Christianity began. Their uncertainty about what would come in evolution, their faith in the ultimate wisdom and strength of the Lord God, teach our souls today how to enter on the way of earthly life facing its dangers, hoping for the fulfilment of its true purpose. In the midst of the succession of stories, a secret treasure of prophecy, a mystery of things to come is found in the Book of Job. It is beyond the comprehension of a child, but the theme will be understood at once, the good man in affliction, the man in torment who can look ahead and sing of the living Redeemer.

The Old Testament unfolds the drama of Man's evolution in the first part of history in great pictures and splendid words. The child's soul strengthens and grows in seeing and hearing them and his power of thought develops as he grapples with the meaning of the stories. He should learn them in the course of years in their proper order, so that in the next stage of his life he will grasp for himself the necessary change from the Old Testament to the New. He should get to know the wording of the Bible as much as the content of the stories. The child's mind grows by encountering much that at first sight cannot be understood. It limits his powers, if he is allowed only cut-down childish versions of Bible stories. He does not in fact need them, if he is given at the correct moment that which belongs rightly to his stage of development. The question could arise here: is it really wise to take children through the main stories of the Old Testament before telling them of the life of Jesus Christ? Must they wait until eleven or twelve years old to know the stories from the Gospels, many of which are gentler and less dramatic than those of the Old Testament?

Naturally children with Christian parents, teachers and ministers to educate them will early hear of Jesus Christ and know something of what is celebrated in the main festivals of the Christian year. But the child's own inner experience of his descent to earth is reflected in the history of Man before the coming of Christ. The drama does not disturb him. It satisfies him to know that his experience is true and real, to admire the heroes, who were great men, even after the gods no longer walked beside them. But a certain stage of inner development, of soul-maturity is needed to enter with feeling and understanding into the life and deed of the Christ. A young child can see the story from outside, but later he will understand it from inside. With the change and progress that should come to him in the eleventh, twelfth, thirteenth years, he should be ripe for the mystery of Man's present and future at the heart of which stands the Christ.

The stories of the Bible, like the Norse, Celtic and Greek myths, lead down into the depths of a world-dilemma, which only God Himself can solve. From the Divine World something must come which has never been known before. The prophets foresaw that God would, must act on earth, if human evolution were to continue. God answered the dilemma by sending Christ, the Son of God, to become man on earth as Jesus. The dramatic events of the Old Testament emerge into the quiet, humble happenings of the Gospels, culminating at the end in the greatest of all dramas on Golgotha, the deed of darkness and light, of death and resurrection. How could the Son of God pass so unnoticed through the world? Why was the world not shaken from the foundations? How could the apostles be weak in faith, the priests strong in hate, the Romans ready to condemn? Why did the peoples of the world who knew themselves to be in the greatest dilemma of history not recognize the God, the Divine Saviour, when He came? To face these questions of religion the child requires an inner strength of soul, which grows in him if he passes rightly and deliberately through what he is taught in earlier years. Then he will approach the mystery of Christianity first of all from outside, as another great story of God and Man, but later with inner understanding of the immense question, which confronts us all our lives from childhood to the end: how do we know the Christ? Many religious people do not even realize how to ask this question even today. Others ask and do not feel that they have found the answer. Still others have begun to discover it and thereby realize that Mankind as a whole is only at the beginning of knowing what Christianity means. The child emerging from childhood encounters the quest of his grown-up years to find the truth of God on earth. His parents, his teachers and his ministers have brought him to the point of experience, from which he can set out to search for himself.

III

THE GROWING CHILD AT PRAYER

PRAYER will have been part of the child's life since he can remember. As soon as he could speak he will have joined in the prayers said for him by the older people and later he will have learnt to say them for himself. As he gets older, he will be able to say longer verses but it is better for him not to be overburdened with any too elaborate form of words. He will be used to praying at night on going to sleep and in the morning on waking up, to saying grace at meals and to offering up a prayer on special important occasions in life. When his school days begin, he will most likely be introduced to prayers said or read by the teachers for the children or by the children for themselves. Learning was at one time always associated with religion and rightly so. There is a big gap in a child's experience, whose lessons have not been preceded by prayer. The child will now have come to the age when he is able to go to church in his own right. He will not be taken along as one of the family, but he will wish to go on his own account. He will begin to realize the prayer of the community as distinct from the private prayers said at home. He may also encounter prayer as a part of the public life of his country. The coronation, for instance, of the kings and queens of England is a religious ceremony held in Church, in which the blessing of God is called down upon the new sovereign, the people of the nation and all its affairs. As the child's experience of the world widens, so he meets the many aspects in the life of prayer, which were previously beyond his ken.

During the years of inner and outer growth which follow the beginning of school-life, the child becomes aware of two worlds extending before him, one outside and the other within his own mind. He feels the powers budding and growing in himself to encounter the new experiences that frequently come from both directions. His relation to prayer should develop in proportion to his changing contact with life itself. The deeper feelings roused in him by the world will bring him into a religious mood that should naturally flow out into prayer. The poet Wordsworth describes such a mood remembered from his own boyhood:

> "for I would walk alone,
> Under the quiet stars, and at that time
> Have felt whate'er there is of power in sound
> To breathe an elevated mood, by form
> Or image unprofaned. . . .
> Thence did I drink the visionary power;
> And deem not profitless those fleeting moods
> Of shadowy exultation: not for this,
> That they are kindred to our purer mind
> And intellectual life; but that the soul,
> Remembering how she felt, but what she felt
> Remembering not, retains an obscure sense
> Of possible sublimity, whereto
> With growing faculties she doth aspire,
> With faculties still growing, feeling still
> That whatsoever point they gain, they yet
> Have something to pursue."
>
> ("The Prelude")

Significantly Wordsworth has recalled this mood from an hour when he was alone. Inwardness of heart will grow best in the child who is allowed to be alone and undistracted from time to time. It has been said in an earlier chapter that loneliness from God is the seed of religion in the human soul. This thought should now be taken further. Prayer in its true meaning should be the blossom growing from the seed of loneliness and the answer to prayer, the sense of God's loving presence, should be its fruit. The art of praying is to approach God so that the answer can be received and felt. What then is the answer for which we look? In one sense we have left the Divine Presence behind at birth. But we can unite with the working of God if we seek for it out of ourselves. The divine forces at work in the world will uphold us, if we recognize them in spirit and in truth. The child's first step in prayer is to realize with reverent understanding how and where they are active, that is to say in all the living creatures around him and in all the people whom he meets. Then he can look at himself and realize that the forces of God live and move in him likewise. If his attitude to the world's creatures, to the bodies and souls of men, is without reverence, if he has been told to see everything in terms of mechanics, he will be unable to fulfil the first condition of prayer. In the world from which we come at birth no disbelief in God is possible, because our very existence is god-given. Here on earth our life is god-given still, but we are not obliged to recognize it in thought. We are at liberty to disbelieve. If however we do so, we know loneliness but no blossom grows from the seed and no fruit from the blossom. If we acknowledge the working of God, we shall feel how the divine forces of the universe continually uphold us, we shall feel ourselves in the hand of God.

There are certain pictures or parables to be found in the Gospels, which describe our life on earth from the point of view, not of ourselves, but of the Divine World. Among them some depict our world on earth as a vineyard from which the owner is trying to reap a harvest of grapes. Human beings are the labourers, God is the owner. Such a picture rouses in our minds the question: what can be supplied here on earth, that the rest of the universe cannot produce? What can God need from us? How can need exist with God? Some answers to these questions can be found, especially if our thoughts remain within the picture. The soil of this vineyard has a special quality, different from that found elsewhere. Divine forces work on earth but the Divine Order does not prevail here as in the other realms of the universe. The labourers have an independence of will unknown to beings in other states of existence. Being independent they can refuse and oppose. But if out of their independence they work with devotion, in sympathy with the owner, they can gather a harvest which will bring the fruit of new life to the universe itself. The heavenly owner values the vineyard for its produce. Man's life on earth is separated from the Presence of God that the fruit of freedom may ripen from independence, and be offered to the Divine World.

Prayer connects us with the true purpose of our existence and the child should approach it in this sense, although no explanation of this kind need be given to him. Experience will show him more than words. As he grows down into this world and finds his independence, he will realize that the god-given powers of mind and body are his to use at will. If he does not pray, he will use them as his own wishes or the dictates of this world require. If he learns to pray truly, he will offer what he has in co-operation with the divine purpose. He will labour out of his own insight to produce the needed harvest. He will not be living for himself alone but as one who knows that he is a citizen of the universe. In prayer he will continually return to the greater purpose and be strengthened in it. He will feel that the higher power of God works into his life and gives it direction. Independent he will be but not god-forsaken because he himself is choosing to seek God.

Prayer should turn the child's mind in reverence towards the being of God and should give him a sense of direction in the use of all his powers. His health of body requires food, air and sleep, and his health of spirit needs regular prayer and thought for religious things. If the former are provided but the latter considered of minor importance, then the child will grow up wild and uncared for in his inner being. It is the custom nowadays to be shocked at neglect to the outer being of a child, at an under-nourished, unkempt appearance or illiterate behaviour. There is nothing like the same attention given to the well-kept, healthy state of the soul. The human being is born from God into the world of earth where, all modern prejudice to the contrary, he never completely belongs. To be true to himself he must constantly turn back to the other part of existence, to the source of his spiritual being. He seeks God because he belongs to the world of Spirit and because his life on earth makes no sense without a spiritual purpose. He is double-natured, born to look heavenward and earthward in equal measure.

How can God be best pictured by a child? Thinking in pictures is natural throughout childhood and his religious life should be filled with them. A grown-up person may be content with a vague idea of the Divine, or even with an abstract principle of

77

divinity, but a child must have and will make pictures. At this point, when grown-ups face the natural needs of children, the whole problem of modern religion, its character and limitations, rises up to confront them. The fact is that we have now reached the last stage of a long process through which religion has been getting more and more vague and uncertain and thereby losing strength. If religion is to give to people of all ages that which they need for true and healthy human living, its meaning and content must be found anew. The idea of God must rise again out of the vague mist into which it has sunk. If we look backwards in history into the Middle Ages and still further back, we shall find that people were aware of a whole world of divine beings, taking part in different ways in human life. In the Christian religion they were called the Hierarchies in nine ranks, the Angels, the Archangels and all the company of Heaven. In other religions different names have been and are still given to them. In later times the feeling for the Divine World of spiritual beings dimmed down, leaving the single vague idea of God. This was a necessary process of history, because Mankind is developing from stage to stage of evolution and consciousness cannot remain at one level. People had to lose their immediate feeling for the spiritual beings around them, and to be left on their own at a certain point. In ordinary life something similar happens, when a young person leaves home and school and goes out alone into the world. His parents, relations and teachers do not cease to exist, but his relationship to them changes, they drop into the background of his consciousness because of the new contacts he has to make as a grown-up. But if his life goes rightly, he will one day turn back to those who guided him in earlier years and find a fresh, working connection with them. He will have left them as child and pupil and will return as friend and helper.

Mankind has historically been in process of going out into the world to stand on his own feet since the close of the Middle Ages. Now the time has come to turn again to the world of divine beings, to rediscover them and start creating the new friendship of the future. Children will not be able to grasp this historical event until they emerge into adolescence. They live with the feeling, that their earlier ancestors had before them, that angels and archangels watch over them and guide their ways. The grown-ups will recognize that this is indeed a fact, for children really live at an earlier stage of historical development in many respects. But the grown-ups will not honestly be able to give to the children the picture of the world of divine beings, unless they realize for themselves how true it is and how necessary it is now to discover it anew in a modern sense. Out of the understanding which has just been outlined, it is possible in all honesty to say to a child who is to sleep in a room alone: Your guardian Angel is watching over you and holds your star over your head, you can speak to him. At the same time the grown-up can say to himself, your guardian Angel will not interfere with you, but he watches to prevent harm coming to you; consult him and he will help you, for he holds your star over your head.

The Angels have special duties in the universe, the care of a single person is assigned to each one. They are the nearest to Man of the nine ranks of beings for whom the old Greek titles are traditionally used in the Christian religion. The Archangels have the care of the people in groups, especially as nations. The Archai watch over epochs of Time, and are the spiritual makers of history. The Exousiai, Dynamis and Kyriotetes work in the forces of Nature outside us and in the weaving of the forces of soul inside human beings. The highest three, the Thrones, the Cherubim and Seraphim, provide the cosmic powers that uphold the world, and drive forward the evolution of Man. The child's picture of the Divine World should include the spiritual beings in their ranks and capacities, each serving God after his kind. Those grown-ups, who can realize the connection, will observe that human customs reflected at one time knowledge of the nine Hierarchies. A reminder is still left in the traditional arrangements of ranks and office in the Church and in the Army.

Where in this picture comes God Himself? He is the one Father of all, in whom the divine beings live, move and have their being. In Him, past, present and future flow together, in whom the origin and the purpose are united. We human beings are children of the heavenly Father and the spiritual beings are the elder brothers of the same family. Such an idea of God may bring about a picture of an infinitely wise, immeasurably old man, whose white hair shows the greatness of age, not its feebleness. There is no harm to the child's mind in this. Many wonderful pictures were painted in the Middle Ages by religious artists on these lines. God is old in the sense of timeless. He is a man in the sense of the Father. He is white-haired for wisdom and His arms spread wide to hold the multitude of His family. They are outstretched in loving care for all that is in the world.

A further question will follow naturally. Where is the place of Christ in this picture? Later on when the child has grown into adolescence, it will be time to bring to him the idea of the Trinity. But he should know the picture of Christ before he comes so far in thought. Christ stands at the threshold of the World of the Spirit and the world of earth. He is the highest Son of God and the Divine Brother of men. He came from the heights of Heaven and made the earth His dwelling. He went through death and rose again to be the Guardian Spirit of all Mankind. When people look right through into each other's hearts, seeing through the outer shell of appearance, they find the Spirit of Christ there. When they look into the depths of their own hearts, they find His presence likewise. The mystery of Christ which should be shown to the child is the paradox that He belongs to the Divine World but He is to be found on earth, that He is the Son of God, but He is the hidden treasure in the human heart. The child will understand the picture of the Divine Father because of his forgotten memories of the life before birth and he will want to grasp the picture of the Divine Son, because he feels in it the mystery, which he will discover for himself in the future.

The picture of God, as it has been described up to this point, has everything in it to give and to rouse love. But what of the fear, which is the great opposite experience of childhood? Where is Evil to be seen? Among the company of spiritual beings who are within the Divine World, some work against the will of God Himself. All beings are in process of development but some of them do not attain to their next stage at the due time. They fall behind and continue their development in an irregular manner, becoming thereby spirits of hindrance and opposition. Evil influences work through them into our life on earth. Fear is the child's first experience of Evil's threat and the contrast between love and fear shows him the spiritual conflict which goes on in the world continually. In prayer he can join with the forces of the Light that withstand the powers of Darkness. He can feel himself taking part in the great cosmic struggle for the Good which is fought out on the battlefield of the earth.

The attempt has been made to describe something of the function of prayer during the years of childhood. The forms of prayer used will depend on the choice of parents, ministers and teachers and eventually of the growing child himself. It is not necessary to change the form of prayer very often, for the truest things of life should be lasting, to be returned to amidst the ups and downs, the joys and sorrows. But those who care for the child's development will judge by an inner sense of tact, when it is right to help him forward to a fresh, more grown-up stage. The familiar prayer need not be left out but a new one can be added. The right adjustment will have to be made between what is bestowed upon him by older people and what he wishes to find for himself. As long as childhood lasts, which is at least up to the age of fourteen, he should be able to feel that a lead is taken by the grown-ups. It is, for instance, a good custom to make a special gift of a form of prayer, new to the child, at an important moment, at one of the religious festivals or on a birthday. Either parents, minister or teacher may undertake to make the solemn presentation. At the same time, as he gets older he may well choose a prayer that particularly attracts him. But this is not a sign that the matter should be entirely left to himself. He will want to feel the warm interest, the wise leadership, which is shown when the grown-ups also choose for him from their wider experience.

No harm will come from words of prayer being said that are beyond the child's immediate grasp. The most widely said of all prayers is the Lord's Prayer. Many of those who love it will feel that all through life they will be finding meaning in its words, which they had missed before. Children are stimulated to grow in understanding if they learn to say words which open the prospect of a lifetime of deepening experience before them. But the right moment should be found when their feeling is ripe for that which is still beyond their powers of thought. In the tenth year of age, a child usually takes a distinct stride forward in consciousness, reaching out to the grown-up existence ahead of him. This offers a natural opportunity to introduce him to, perhaps, the Lord's Prayer, which belongs not to childhood, but to the whole of his life to come. The guiding thought inspiring the necessary tact in the grown-ups should be to help the child to grow in the ability to pray, as he develops his other capacities. Prayer should be grown into, not grown out of as childhood is gradually left behind. Two dangers threaten in this respect. Out of the embarrassment or helplessness of the grown-ups the child may be left alone with his life of prayer too soon and may abandon it altogether. Or the early forms may be continued too long and prayer itself may come to seem childish.

Some people feel a natural wish to make their own personal forms of prayer. This habit easily begins in childhood. It can be part of the problem described in an earlier chapter of making petitions for wishes to be fulfilled and dangers averted. Here the thought of the guardian Angel can be of help. He stands near to our personal concerns and watches over the best part of our being. Before the age of personal responsibility he can exert a great influence over what happens to the child of his care. Later on, he must limit himself to preventing and warning against harm. But at all times, he can be called upon and consulted. When a child wishes to carry on his private conversation with a higher being, he may be directed to his guardian Angel. Later in life he will find much assistance from thinking of what his Angel's point of view might be and asking for his help. When praying for other people, it is important to look for the link with their guardian spirits, that the loving thoughts of human hearts may join with the strength of the Angels.

Story-telling at bedtime is a valuable custom in the early part of childhood. As the child grows beyond it, the mother, father or both, perhaps even the whole family, can begin to read together in the evenings with the children. The first thought for many people will be to read passages from the Bible. It is one thing to learn the stories as lessons and quite another to read aloud from the Psalms, the books of the Prophets, then later from the Gospels and Epistles. The holy words will become part of the child's inner being if they are heard again and again, read as an act of worship. The family conversations, that may come about in this quiet time, will bring a natural sharing of religious experience. Religion is not entirely a matter for one's self, but can profitably be shared. It may sound at times in these pages as if the needs of the single child might be difficult to meet in a family with children at different ages and stages. In fact, it can do them no harm to bear with and allow for each other's requirements. But a child who is growing into his teens will be feeling the need for some privacy. Then, again with tact, the others in the family should be willing to let him have it, to leave him to read the Bible for himself and to say his own prayers. He can join in that which belongs to the family as a community and be alone with that which is his individual concern.

Prayer is that which makes our human life on earth worthy of beings who belong to the World of Spirit as much as to this world. The child is aware of his spiritual inheritance by a feeling which Wordsworth, the poet of childhood, could express like this:

"Our birth is but a sleep and a forgetting:
The Soul that rises with us, our life's Star,
   Hath had elsewhere its setting,
   And cometh from afar:
   Not in entire forgetfulness,
   And not in utter nakedness,
   But trailing clouds of glory do we come
   From God, who is our home:
Heaven lies about us in our infancy!
Shades of the prison-house begin to close
   Upon the growing Boy,
But he beholds the light, and whence it flows
   He sees it in his joy;
The Youth, who daily farther from the East
   Must travel, still is Nature's Priest,
   And by the vision splendid
   Is on his way attended;
At length the Man perceives it die away,
And fade into the light of common day."

But, though the growing child cannot keep the inheritance as it was, it can be transformed. The spiritual treasure within himself can be sought and found, through which he can pray. His heart will be lifted up by the power of his own spirit to find the Spirit of God.

BETWEEN GOOD AND EVIL

"Weren't you bad?" said the little girl in an awed voice. The Nativity Play was over and outside in the entrance hall she had encountered an actor still in costume. His part had been that of a cruel, greedy innkeeper, who had refused lodging to Mary and Joseph in Bethlehem because they were poor. The contrast had struck home into the child's heart between the man out for himself and the homeless couple, whose child was born amongst the beasts in the stable because there was no room for them in the inn. She was deeply satisfied to have seen so clearly the difference between good and evil.

"She's had it," came the voice of the little boy cutting across the quiet of a spellbound audience. The puppets wobbled uncertainly, for those who pulled the strings from above were far from skilled. But one moment of drama had been successfully achieved. Persephone, the daughter of the Greek goddess Demeter, had picked the forbidden flower and Pluto, the god of the underworld, had arrived promptly to snatch her away into his kingdom. The little boy had come in an unfriendly mood to the performance and watched at first with many shufflings of feet. But the story had gripped him after all and when the climax was reached, he was carried away to the point of shouting out aloud its moral.

Children are acutely aware of the contrast between good and bad. They look for the moral drama in every story and react to it in every situation. But they want clear-cut distinctions and suffer very much when they are left uncertain and confused. They have an inborn moral feeling but they have to learn how to use it in the conditions of this world, which they are getting bit by bit to know. Their own powers are something they cannot estimate until they learn by experience. A child cannot tell how strong he is, how loud his voice is, how much noise he is making, how much damage he is doing until the consequences show him. The phrase "I didn't mean to" is very often not an excuse but a statement of fact. But the conditions of the world outside themselves are equally unknown to children. They have to learn to be aware of their own behaviour and to adjust it to the requirements of the world. But while they learn, the essential distinction between good and bad has always to be made. Life is full of puzzles in childhood.

Is the child born good or does he start life with all the criminal tendencies there are? Historically this is a very old question but it has emerged in modern psychology as if it had never been known before. It arises from the experience which anyone will have who observes himself honestly. He will notice that the tendency to every bad motive and to every type of wrong-doing can be found in himself. When he hears of crimes, he will have to admit that under certain circumstances he also might have committed them. The difference between himself and the criminal lies in the fact that he has not acted on his tendencies but the other one has done so. This might be due to greater strength of character, or to better upbringing and less tempting circumstances. The old saying rises in his heart: "There but for the grace of God, go I." Nevertheless he can find in himself an innate sense of goodness. He feels freer and stronger in his being, when he is aware of having spoken the truth, acted out of compassion and upheld the good. The question is: which has come first, which is essential to his human nature, the good in him or the tendencies to the bad?

In these pages the picture has been drawn of the child born in innocence. This particular answer to our question is supported by the natural feeling of joy and reverence, which we have for the small baby. We shall find reverence of another kind for the person at the other end of life, for the dying and the dead. Death brings to sight the nobility of being, which is often hidden in ordinary life. Naturally there is another side to the picture of being born and of dying, the element of struggle and anxiety and the burden of physical distress. But in another sense birth and death reveal the higher part of human nature. The soul is born in innocence and departs in nobility. In between the two gates of existence he encounters the forces that make for wickedness. The child acquires forces and develops tendencies on his way into life, through which his innocence becomes mixed with badness. He shows himself to have an already formed character, which he has brought with him and which emerges as his means of expression develop. This itself is a mixture of good and bad qualities. The child who was born knowing the Good, enters as he grows into the knowledge of Evil and thereby into the struggle between them, into which man is caught in his life on earth. The child knows this to be a fact of experience. He does not need teaching about the Fall of Man, except in the sense of providing him with a picture and a story to illustrate what he is already aware of himself. But he requires and asks for moral training, that is to say help in handling his own forces and dealing with the conditions of the world, so that his original good can triumph over what is naturally bad. As soon as he grasps the drama of earth-existence, he recognizes that it is played between the powers of Good and Evil. The child has a moral feeling about Life, which as a grown-up, he may later suppress, but which in childhood is his most vivid experience.

It is neither necessary nor wise to play down the existence of objective Evil to spare the child's feelings. He may be a child with regard to means of expression but he knows more than his few years have taught him. The fundamental facts of existence are clear to him in the manner in which wisdom naturally lives in a child's heart and he will only be perplexed if they are not acknowledged openly. It is a matter of expressing them in the picture-thoughts that he can grasp without overstraining his mind. He will want to know about the Devil, to see pictures of him and perhaps watch him in plays on the stage. The Devil will have his throng of followers, demons expert in wickedness of all kinds. The child will realize himself that there are personal devils, serving the great powers of Evil, as truly as there are guardian Angels, acting as the messengers of God. With the realistic logic of childhood, he will know that if there are good spirits helping us, there are likewise elements of hindrance. We cannot have one without the other.

Courage to stand for the Good is the most needed of virtues

in our day. The child has the best chance of developing this quality, who is neither falsely guarded against knowing about Evil, nor made afraid by too many warnings or threats. Out of himself a child takes life seriously, however gaily he may behave, and is well able to appreciate the struggle of Good and Evil. It gives him the opportunity to take part in something that really matters. Let him know of the Archangel Michael and he will be anxious to be one of his helpers. Each Archangel has his own character and special mission. Gabriel holds, in the traditional representations, the lily in his hand, Raphael the staff of healing and Michael the sword. In the old pictures he is shown with the dragon at his feet, whom he is in the process of overcoming. He has long been regarded as the helper of Man against the power of Evil. A stern silent Being compared with the other Archangels, nevertheless a large number of holy places and churches have been dedicated to him. He is known for his special concern over Mankind's future on earth and was sometimes shown by earlier artists carrying on his arm a small human figure, the representative of Man. The dragon under his feet is never depicted dead, for the power of Evil is not to be annihilated, but overcome, and, by the strength of the Spirit, transformed. The growing child is particularly able to appreciate the heroic figure of this Archangel and to realize that his own personal struggles are part of the great world-conflict of Good and Evil.

The moral training of children should be set against a heroic background such as this, for so they themselves will understand and appreciate it. This may seem a strange claim to make for the minds of the children. But one fact of experience is widely recognized at present, that the behaviour of many young people is so unsatisfactory as to be a serious social problem. What went wrong with their upbringing is the perplexed question involved. One answer, which is put forward in all seriousness here, is that too little was expected of them in the years of growth, when they inwardly longed to see life in heroic proportions. Some may have been left to behave as they liked, others will have been asked to behave nicely or like other people. Still others may have been presented with a set of rules or a code of what is done or not done. None of them, treated in any of these ways, will have been made to feel that their thoughts, sayings and doings are as morally important as they themselves would wish them to be. What, for instance, are the stories that interest children? Fairy stories are always a drama of those who serve the Good against the bad. The witch is defeated in the end and the good prince and princess, their trials surmounted, live happily ever after. The legends of heroes, like King Arthur and his knights, tell how they fought bravely against oppressors, witches and dragons. The minds of children are hungry for tales that illustrate the dramatic struggle of Good against Evil. But children are not by nature onlookers. They at once take part, even if it is only by repeating what interests them in play. They feel part of the great drama they so readily understand. As soldiers of Michael, they will help to put the dragon underfoot.

The child has his own innate sense for the reality of Good and Evil but he will depend on the grown-ups to show him how to behave well. He has to learn how to deal with his own nature and the condition of the world around. The grown-ups are responsible for his training. The objection might be raised to what is said in these pages that all children are made to sound alike, that they are often gathered together under the one heading: "the child". This is however in fact true to life. Children are very varied in character and background but remarkably alike in the trend of their development. Each particular child at each stage of growth is a variation on a common theme. What is here put forward are some general principles, which could prove useful guiding thoughts for the upbringing of many individual children, with their special characters. Those who have the responsibility of bringing them up will see the guiding thoughts according to the needs of the particular children they have under their care.

Growing children will be found to appreciate goodness as beautiful and wickedness as ugly. Their moral feelings tend to be artistic and they will readily understand this line of approach. Told that some piece of behaviour is wrong, they may ask why. When they hear that it is dark and ugly, they will respond out of their own hearts without question. In one part of our minds, in which we are usually only half awake, we all tend to estimate our feelings artistically. Anger make us "see red" in hot dancing flames, or it turns into sharp icicles of cold wrath. Jealousy puts a bilious green haze over our life's scene and distorts its pictures. Fear draws hard lines round what we see and throws the details into sharp relief or in another mood puts everything into a fuddle of mixed-up colours. Joy and anticipation glaze over all we see with a sparkling light. Our actions can be felt in the same way. A deed of kindness brings warm sunshine among those who share in it, but a mean piece of selfishness is as chilling as frost. Listening to another person so that he feels inwardly understood sets a light glowing but arguing past each other brings swirls of fog into the situation. How differently does a day begin! Sometimes a clear light shines, the sense of purpose is bright and goodwill is in the air but the clouds of muddle soon gather and the fumes of bad feeling begin to rise. Another day will start in a cloud of apprehension, difficulties threatening at every turn and a chill wind of criticism blowing. But with determination the sunshine is called out. When we notice as grown-ups this aspect of experience, we can become more aware of the child's sense of things. Looking back to the years of childhood it is often easier to remember the colour and climate of a situation than what brought it about.

The child learns moral lessons by experiencing life in this manner. The poet Wordsworth, who was much inspired in his writings by memories of boyhood, was often able to describe how an outwardly simple experience on an outing amongst the lakes and hills, where he grew up, formed his character. The boy, who amused himself shouting lustily in a valley where the hills echoed back his cries, would sometimes hear in the pauses a powerful force of silence moving down upon him from the still and ancient peaks. When he stole a boat on the lake one summer evening and rowed out alone over the water, he saw coming into view over the crags the mighty slope of the mountain like a figure of divine judgement. On a bright autumn day, he went gathering hazel nuts and came into a little wood that no one but he had yet discovered. The beauty and quiet sank into his heart, but then, greedy for the nuts, he began to pull at the branches. The contrast between the untouched beauty of the place and the devastation he caused by his own action struck him horribly.

"the shady nook
Of hazels and the green and mossy bower,
Deformed and sullied, patiently gave up
Their quiet being. . . .
Ere from the mutilated bower I turned
Exulting, rich beyond the wealth of kings,
I felt a sense of pain when I beheld
The silent trees and saw the intruding sky.
Then, dearest Maiden, move along these shades
In gentleness of heart; with gentle hand
Touch—for there is a spirit in the woods."

When a child can be at liberty to make his experiences by himself with the living world of Nature, he will learn as much about morality as natural history. In fact, as long as fewer people were brought up in towns and the country was more accessible, some problems of behaviour were simpler. But nowadays we have to replace from within very much of that which was once given to people from outside, and not only because of circumstances. The Book of Job in the Old Testament describes, on the one hand, how powerfully the working of God in Nature was felt by people of old time. They knew the moral significance of every living thing. But when they turned to look at man, they met a question without an answer. The book, on the other hand, shows us the fate of Job who is righteous but must suffer. In his suffering, he challenges God with the unanswered question. It would be true to say that we are still discovering the answer today. In a practical way, we encounter the fact that Nature alone does not morally educate us sufficiently for our needs, because man has problems that go beyond what she knows. Nature can help children, but cannot replace what they must learn from older people.

The child will learn by his artistic sense the beauty of what is good and the ugliness of what is bad. This sense will naturally be directed towards what people are and what they do, more than to what they preach. Telling the child what is right has much less effect than example. It has been pointed out in earlier chapters how strong in small children is the impulse to imitate. In older children the capacity for imitation becomes more inward and more moral. It unites with the developing ability to discriminate. The child longs to imitate but looks for behaviour worthy of being imitated, for that which expresses what is good, true and beautiful. He looks for a hero, someone greater, wiser, more controlled and more worthy than himself, to admire, to serve and to copy. His soul is growing like his body and needs a model to emulate and standards to reach. Hero-worship is a necessity in his life for some years. In grown-up people the need to worship those whom they admire can be a sign of immaturity or weakness of character. But in children it is a symptom of healthy growth and should be guarded from being misunderstood. It can, for instance, be very harmful to destroy by criticism a child's hero, to demonstrate, in an old phrase, that the idol has feet of clay. Parents who have been accustomed to be all in all to the little child may receive a great shock when, on growing older, he turns from them to a strange hero. Or they may have cause to fear the example which he has chosen for himself. To abstain from criticism may ask for considerable self-restraint but for the sake of the child's moral training, it is necessary. Instead of trying to expose the hero for what he is they can make efforts to replace him. The child's moral good taste is usually reliable. If the opportunity is given for finding a worthier hero, he will be glad to take it.

The favourite stories of growing children, as was observed earlier on, are dramas of the struggle between Good and Evil in fairy story, legend and history. But children do not enjoy looking on, they want to take part. They expect the real life around them to be in the same mould as the stories. They look for their favourite heroes among the people they know as much as those found in the book. By their attitude to life, they say, though not in so many words, to those they meet: when are you going to be like King Arthur, where can I find Galahad, who has hidden the Lady of the Lake, will Merlin be here tomorrow? But the grown-ups may well be modest folk, not expecting much of themselves, having forgotten their own childhood and not expecting to be above the ordinary. They bring intense disappointment to the child if they cannot show him anything heroic in themselves.

He needs heroes, to respect, venerate and encounter with awe. Where is he to find them? The most powerful element in moral education is the quest for the hero and the greatest failure on the part of the grown-ups is not to provide him.

It is clear that heroes are only available if at least some of the older people known to the child ask very much of themselves. Circumstances cannot make them heroic but only the qualities cultivated from within have the power to do so. The child will appreciate someone who has learnt for himself many things that he was not taught. He will notice who can do something that requires skill and act with cleverness as well as strength. He will want to be shown how another person has overcome a limitation, been patient with a hard fate, faced failure without failing. In childish ignorance, his first admiration may be for outer show and physical strength. But he can learn to refine his power to admire and turn from the outer to the inner. He will want to develop in himself what he reveres in his chosen heroes. Children in their longing to worship expect to see life lived in a grand heroic style which many grown-ups might think unreasonable. But they want in their hearts much also to be expected of them and are grateful to parents and teachers who ask a high standard of effort and behaviour. Spoilt children tend to feel that no one finds it important how they behave, and, all appearance to the contrary, resent the absence of discipline.

Where the child feels respect and confidence in the grown-ups he will be willing to obey and accept rules of behaviour. The child has by nature the good sense to realize that he has not yet developed the powers in himself to decide what is to be done and to make good use of his forces. The way in which some children behave might well lead to doubt about how much confidence should be put in their fundamental good sense. But if something really important happens, if an emergency arises, the same children will often make quite a different showing. The child expects the demand for his obedience and the strength of discipline to come from the grown-ups. He waits for the reign of law and order to be imposed from above, that he can adapt himself to it. Of course he reserves the right to kick against it, to wheedle for the special treat. By their very nature, rules can be broken. But this does not mean that he is against order and obedience. They are the much needed firm background to the changing, disturbing course of his experiences. Where there is no discipline at home and at school, children do not thrive. But the effort to produce order and demand obedience has to come from the grown-ups. If they lack the insight to see how necessary it is or the strength of character to insist, the children lose confidence.

The child expects authority from older and wiser people but only until he will have grown capable of finding the inner power to become responsible for himself. He hopes that they will show him how to develop to this stage. Meanwhile he is glad to leave the responsibility to them. But he is demanding very much more that they would have expected to ask of themselves. He looks to them to call for his sake upon the spiritual powers, which he hopes later to find from within. It was earlier suggested that the picture of the Archangel Michael, Man's defender against the dragon of Evil, would appeal powerfully to the mind of the child. But the grown-ups should understand the character of this spiritual guardian of Man still more deeply and realistically. They should feel what it means to have courage in the face of temptation, to uphold truth where lying is easier, to put integrity before success. In every such effort, an individual person is joining his forces to those of the Archangel Michael, to withstand the threat of Evil in the affairs of our own time. Someone who has experienced this can point the way into life to a young child with an authority that comes of itself.

Some of the best modern thoughts on the nature of the child are found in the books of Rudolf Steiner. He has shown how each age brings a different stage of consciousness and what should be given to the child at each one. He has composed prayers for children and given advice on what they should be taught. His suggestions have outstanding value because they are derived from the ideal of the complete fully-grown man in relation to the world of the earth and the world of the Spirit, to both of which he belongs at once. The training of children has its source in the grown-ups. The more complete a human being is, the more he can teach the child how to behave in his struggle between Good

94

and Evil. The higher his ideal of man, the higher will be his standard of morals. The grown-up is the child's hero and the model which he seeks to imitate. The ideas of Rudolf Steiner can help the grown man to know himself in his full human dignity that the child can follow the example. By nature every child wants to grow into a man or woman but there is no natural answer to the grown-up question: what is man, how can I become fully human? The answer can be found only by spiritual understanding, by the effort of mind that reaches beyond what Nature provides. It is this effort that the child expects from the grown-up whom he has chosen to admire and to follow.

V

HOLDING SERVICES

THE service for the children was over and the family had settled
down again at home. The little girl took out the coloured pencils
and drew a picture of the service and presented it to the minister.
She attended a place of worship where candles were lighted on
the altar and the seven flames were the background. In front
stood the robed minister and at the side the assistant. The figure
of the minister was drawn very large, great blue eyes burnt in
the face and flames of golden hair streamed from the head. The
assistant was represented by a small figure in subdued colours.
In the foreground of the drawing stood a row of children seen
from the back, very small figures before the huge one of the
minister. It was a very gay picture, expressing the child's satis-
faction with what she had seen, and was presented as if to say
"thank you". In real life the minister was a smaller person than
the assistant, with dark hair instead of golden, and the children
by no means tiny. The picture was not an outer portrait but the
expression of an inner experience. The proportions of size were in
fact close to those that can be seen in a painting from an ancient
Egyptian temple, in which the gods are shown instructing human
beings. The gods are large majestic figures and the people small
and modest. The size represents the greatness of the divine wisdom
compared with that of men.

In her drawing the little girl had made the figure of the minister
the symbol for her religious experience. Yellow was the dominat-
ing colour and streaming lines like sunbeams were the centre of the
design. Looking at the picture, one could have said, for this child
the Spirit shines like the sun and she rejoices in it as much as
anyone seeing outer sunshine after cloudy weather. A further
thought could be taken from this childish drawing and one could
say: so a service of worship should be, the spiritual sun should

shine into the hearts of those present, that they themselves may shine on earth with divine light.

Children experience very much through the eyes. They will begin to understand the purpose of churchgoing, if they have the opportunity to see church buildings and become acquainted with the different types of architecture used in the past. So they will begin to understand how people in other times worshipped God. Where it is difficult to visit actual buildings, photographs and pictures can be very useful. Many experiences will come about by this means, of which one can be described here by way of example. The Gothic church was the type evolved during the later Middle Ages, which has so often been copied since that it represents the general idea of a Christian place of worship. In shape it is like a cross laid out on the ground. From the centre rises a tower, topped often with a steeple. The houses of the town are grouped round it like attendants round an important person. If the town is approached from the distance, the church spire is seen from far off. Churches have often been built near the sea, so that the sailors returning in their ships saw them from afar and were guided home. Inside the church, beneath its high arches, people find themselves in a different world from that outside. There is a feeling of quiet and space. The eyes are drawn upwards away from the little things near at hand. The windows may be made of coloured glass, filling the space with another kind of light than that outside. Sounds come harmoniously between the arches, and everyone avoids making ordinary sharp noises. There is much to see, the altar at the east end, pictures, carvings, words inscribed on the walls, all directing the thoughts away from the bustle of the world outside to heavenly things. Memorials to the dead are here, for they are remembered not as the tiresome characters they may well have been in daily life, but in the true grandeur of soul in which everyone may partake under the shadow of eternity. Sitting quietly in an empty church, thoughts change, feelings become deeper and more reverent. When the congregation is present and the service begins, the church fills with the sound of music, with voices singing, and with the solemn fall of holy words read aloud. The world within the church has come alive. Ordinariness has ceased for a while and as

97

the arches appear to reach in space towards Heaven, time seems to float towards the eternal. The hearts are lifted up and the wings of the angelic company sound to listening ears. The beauty of holiness, as it is called in the Psalms, has become real for the moment.

The child needs to experience a holy place and a holy time, that holiness may become a real thing to him in life. Not everyone today knows what this word can mean. Some people are embarrassed by a solemn atmosphere, or dislike to hear words said without a personal note. They become angry if their hearts are lifted away from ordinary things. Children are not usually so troubled. They naturally appreciate the dignity of behaviour that should go with a holy place and a holy time. They enjoy taking part in solemn events and will rarely behave badly during a ceremony such as a wedding. But their natural gift should be educated that the meaning of what is holy can be found by them again in later life at a deeper level. In childhood a natural need is present for the outward expression of an inward feeling. Holiness should live in certain times, places and things. Among the Puritans, who on principle abstained from making their places of worship or their services beautiful, special reverence was shown for "The Book". By this they meant the Bible, and in many families of this persuasion the holy volume lay on a table by itself in a quiet part of the best room. It would never have been found in a pile among other books. A child can well understand such a custom expressing the reverence in which the Holy Book was held. Many a one who has just learnt to read and has been given his own copy of the Bible will without question keep it apart and would be shocked at himself if he found that he had put another book on top of it. The child's feeling for holiness needs such means of expression, which should be accepted and respected by older people.

At one end of New York's Wall Street stands a church complete with spire in the traditional style. As it is not far from the waterfront, it must once have been seen above the surrounding houses from the distance by those who approached Manhattan from across the water. Now enormous skyscrapers stand on either side, so close that it can only be seen at one angle from down the street. What was once a commanding spire reaches with its highest tip only part way up the walls towering on either side. Inevitably it makes a startling impression to see how far the buildings representing finance have overtopped the church. In Biblical language, one would say that the temples of Mammon have outstripped the Temple of God. By contrast, there are old-fashioned cities in Europe so crowded with old churches and monasteries that it seems as if in earlier centuries there must have been little room for anything except religion. In such a contrast the historical situation can be seen into which the children of today grow up. The traditional kind of religion has a long history, but belongs for the most part to the past, which, wonderful as it was, cannot be brought back except in empty imitations. The present civilization does not appear to need religion, or at least much that is important in its affairs functions successfully without it. What are the children to do with such a situation?

It has been suggested that children can learn how holiness was expressed in the past and two examples have been given, the atmosphere in an old church and the reverent handling of the Bible as a book. But they should realize as they grow up that we cannot now live in what the past gives to us. We can complete its history and learn from it but we must then look towards the future. Religion must needs take a different place in life from that which it used to do, for people have changed their outlook and their customs. Once upon a time, and for some it is still so, religion was chiefly part of the social life of the neighbourhood, the city, the nation. Whatever someone might believe in his heart, he took part. An Oriental coming to the West once asked why religion was shut up in church buildings and kept for one day of the week. In his home country religious processions took place in the streets, public celebrations were all derived from the customs of the temple and social conventions had a sacred meaning. In the past the same could have been said of the West. The greeting of farewell "Good-bye" was originally "God be with you", but today an agnostic would say it without a second thought. Religion and ordinary life have parted company and the growing child, to whom the old style of life would be more natural, has to find his way into the new state of affairs. Has religion become unimportant? The answer to this question is a divided one. In the old style it is disappearing before the demands of outer civilization as the church is among the skyscrapers in Wall Street. But it can come to life again within the hearts of men and women. When the outer life was more religious than it is now, there were some people who conformed to what was expected and others who were filled with inner devotion. Nowadays religion belongs much more than before to the inner place of the soul. The Canadian minister who wrote recently, "We have a clubby, chubby church" was saying in fact, we have a church without much religion. But the historical situation of today is an important opportunity. We can decide to turn from the outer to the inner, from social custom to the worship of God in spirit and in truth. True religion today depends upon the awakening of the spirit within the human soul to seek the Divine Spirit of the World.

The religious life of children cannot be the same as that of the grown-ups, because their inner experience is different. This is no hindrance to their taking part in the things which they cannot inwardly grasp. They have their own way of learning by experience. They can be taught to take part on public occasions, to be present at a wedding, a christening or even a funeral, as they might also be required to attend functions at school or in the town. They can sit through a church service for grown-ups if need be. If they are bored or protest, the members of the family or other people will decide what to do about it. But for the development of the soul in childhood, it is not harmful to be present on an occasion beyond the child's grasp, provided that he is allowed to look on and find his own kind of interest. He should not be asked to take an inner part, nor required to be present at any service for grown-ups where inner participation is necessary, such as the Christian Eucharist. But it is important for the child's training for life to accept the needs of the grown-ups in their world, as they should respect what he needs in his. Give and take between the generations will benefit everyone.

With this necessary qualification, the point can now be made that, the inner experience of a child being different from that of the grown-up, this should be allowed for in religious matters.

Both children and grown-ups need holy occasions, holy times and holy places. The prayers said at home are not sufficient after the first few years. But the children need for their own sake services of a different kind from those in which the grown-ups can participate. This is not to say that they require services cut down to small size or simplified for childish minds. They need what is different in the sense that their inner experience is different. Children grow morally by admiring someone beyond their own level. They thrive spiritually by growing towards something that they do not at first comprehend. How can they develop in understanding, if they have no chance to ask: what does this mean? what are these words saying? How can they grow in spirit, if they never have an experience, which they hope to grasp better in time to come than they can at present? They need as big, as universal an idea of God as the grown-ups. They should become familiar with outer words and customs that clothe the inner spiritual realities. But the distinction should be made that they can only see outside, beyond themselves, that which later on, as grown-ups, they should find within. The child's soul is still on the way down into the body. It is felt by him to be around and above him while another part of his being, the self, is alto-gether hidden in the future. He grows towards this mysterious part of himself, which he will one day meet and receive into his inner life.

> "And I have felt
> A presence that disturbs me with the joy
> Of elevated thoughts, a sense sublime
>
> . . . .
>
> A motion and a spirit, that impels
> All thinking things, all objects of all thought
> And rolls through all things."   (Tintern Abbey)

Wordsworth, from the memory of his youth, calls up this mood of feeling for the Spirit, that breathes through the world and will, as the child grows to manhood, waken within his soul as his spiritual sense of self. That which at first he beheld in the world beyond, he will then find within, as his individual treasure of spirit.

A practical illustration may be added from the life of the Christian Church. At a certain age, in some denominations earlier, in some later, but rightly speaking about the age of fourteen, the child is confirmed. After this ceremony, he is admitted to the Communion Service and receives the bread and wine. Previously, he is a child in the life of the Church, and afterwards he has the privileges of a grown-up. In most religions the passing from childhood to youth is given a sacred celebration, marking the initiation of the growing soul into the world of earth. In Christian practice the receiving of consecrated bread and wine is reserved for those who have outgrown childhood. The question often arises, why the taking of food should be a religious act? Religious experience begins in thinking and feeling, as the soul partakes in the words and the act of offering in the service. Then the deeper level of the will is reached, as the spiritual force that quickens the soul descends to transform the powers of the body. In a grown-up person the soul has moved completely into the bodily house and the self has awakened to independent existence. The spirit that earlier hovered around the child has now arrived within and looks out into the world of earth and up to the world of Heaven. At this stage, when the development to manhood is complete, the human spirit experiences bodily existence and becomes aware of being menaced and dragged down by the power of matter. The longing for redemption rises to consciousness and quickens the insight into the working of Christ. The consecration of bread and wine sets to work the forces of redemption which can penetrate the human being in spirit, soul and body. The communion is the leaven wakening to life the process of transformation through which man will be redeemed.

The child cannot be given the communion because he has not descended deeply enough into material existence to recognize its working. He inwardly looks forward to a future stage of development when the mystery will be revealed to him for which he is not yet ripe. A service for children should answer his inner sense of something greater still to come. It should, speaking symbolically, be held in front of a door that has still to open. The words should so speak to the child that he becomes aware of his own spirit on its way down to live within his body. If these two experiences are created in a service for children, their inner religious feeling will be satisfied. The little girl whose drawing was described at the beginning of the chapter had been to a service in which the children themselves speak once, each on his own, for himself. They promise to seek the Spirit of God. When these words are said the minister gives to each one his hand as the promise is made. The promise and the gesture have the place in the service corresponding to the communion in the Eucharist attended by the grown-ups. The child promises to seek and when he is grown-up he will be able to receive.

The religious life of the child is incomplete, if he does not attend services in church, especially such as are arranged to meet his inner feeling in the way described. Prior to his schooldays, religion in his home life is sufficient. The home becomes only one part in his life as he grows older. He enters the wider community when he attends school to learn and church to worship. But his parents will decide which religion he is to follow, just as they choose in which school he is to be educated. At this stage he has not yet the strength of soul to decide for himself. Some grown-ups like to believe that they are justified in leaving such important decisions to the child. They would not expect him to carry heavy parcels or suitcases until his arms and legs are strong enough but they are willing to put burdens on his soul far beyond his strength. Responsibility lies naturally with the parents during the years of childhood. The child is ready to venture into the world beyond his home but he needs their guidance, until he is mature enough to find the way for himself.

Although the child should join in worship from time to time with children and grown-ups outside the family, this in no way hinders or replaces what may be done at home. Just as the festivals of the year can be celebrated among members of the family, so on a holy day, on Sunday evening for instance, an act of worship can be held. For the most part, parents and children will find out their own form, although there are, in some religions, prescribed ceremonies to be carried out in the circle of home. Where this is not so, reading and singing will prove most valuable. Whereas in church, the children will find the pattern of the service laid down and their own part defined, they will appreciate the opportunity at home to make a contribution they can choose at will. Many will enjoy reading aloud a passage from the Bible of their own choice and listening to what each other, including the grown-ups, can contribute. Singing and music-making will also be chosen according to the attainments and wishes of those present.

There is a charming story from the Middle Ages of a juggler, a humble and poor man, who wished to make an offering to the Madonna, but had nothing to give. He crept at last into an empty church and began to perform on the altar steps the stunts with which he entertained the people in the towns and castles. The priest who discovered him was full of reproaches for such behaviour in church, but the juggler explained that he was offering in the house of God all that he had. Children naturally understand the longing to make an offering of what one has or can do, and they will be able to bring to a simple act of worship at home a grateful devotion. The members of the family, who willy-nilly share all their daily affairs, will come together in an uplifted mood to partake in a solemn moment. They will realize the deeper nature in each other, seeing a glimpse of the eternal soul emerging from the everyday appearance.

The world of every day has claims that cannot be ignored and which the children have to learn in the course of growing up to accept. Chores have to be done, money earned and spent, lessons learned by the children, jobs done by the grown-ups. But the round of existence becomes flat and grey if nothing beyond these preoccupations is considered. Relief can be sought in dreams and in the fantasies of the screen or in more lurid ways. But the human heart, especially the child's heart, longs for the Heavens to open and the divine light to shine in the light of everyday. Holy times, holy places and holy customs lift our life from time to time heavenward. A story is told in the Gospels of two women, Martha, who was very busy with her household affairs, and Mary, who took the time to sit quietly and listen when the divine guest was in their home. Many times the question arises: which shall it be? In reality, we can each be both Martha and Mary, but we should choose the right time for the one and for the other. Both the earthly and the heavenly parts belong to our life on earth. Once upon a time it was considered more important than anything else to build temples or churches. Nowadays the pendulum has swung in the opposite direction. Factories, offices, places of entertainment tend to be the first priority. The time should come to find the balance. The process begins in childhood, when the children are guided to see in life that which is earthly and heavenly in equal proportion.

> "That blessed mood,
> In which the burden of the mystery,
> In which the heavy and the weary weight
> Of all this unintelligible world
> Is lightened . . . .
> Until the breath of this corporeal frame
> And even the motion of our human blood
> Almost suspended, we are laid asleep
> In body, and become a living soul:
> While with an eye made quiet by the power
> Of harmony, and the deep power of joy,
> We see into the life of things."

So Wordsworth has described the longing of the soul for spiritual life. In the practice of religion, in acts of worship, the eternal soul is set free to seek the Divine Spirit in whom we live, move and find our true being.

Part Three

Youth

I

THE NEED FOR GOD

THE boy or girl, leaving childhood behind and stepping into youth, finds before him a world that is continually changing, a fascinating, but confusing world. As a child, he has been through manifold changes, but he had felt himself sheltered by his parents and teachers. In the last resort, their authority has been accepted because they gave protection. Parents and teachers may do badly by the children under their care, they may seem to an onlooker to be making all the mistakes there are, but during the years of childhood, they will, in spite of themselves, be felt as a source of protection. A significant experience is to be met with in boys and girls who are approaching their teens. It will happen sometimes that one of them with a parent, who was not at all what he should have been, will start to defend the father or mother in an unbelievably generous way. A girl who had to be given care and protection by the State was found by a teacher in her school gazing at the photograph of her very unsatisfactory mother. "That's my Mum," she said, "she tries so hard." Another child whose father's unbalanced behaviour was a trial to his whole family said to her grandmother, "I don't think we should expect too much of him." Those who are leaving their childhood behind and stepping beyond the protection they once needed, feel a deep impulse of gratitude although they may not always be able to express it.

At the age of about fourteen, a climax will usually be reached in the process of growing up. One aspect often receives more attention than any other, the oncoming of puberty with all the complications which the forces of sex bring with them. But the change in the nature of the child entering youth is much greater and deeper than just this. Parents and teachers need powers of imagination at every stage of childhood, but they face the biggest test of their wisdom and insight in the years of youth. The young person begins the process of coming into his own, which will of necessity take some years. Human beings differ from animals by needing a long time to grow up. Those who are accustomed to observe them know how soon the kitten becomes a cat, the calf a cow, the lamb a sheep compared with the human baby becoming a grown-up person. Once the animal is fully grown, development ceases; the pattern is fulfilled and only the process of ageing continues. The sheep is predestined to go on being a sheep, while the cow, the pig, the horse do likewise. The human being, by comparison, goes through a slow and complicated process of growing up and when he is physically mature, he remains capable of unforeseeable, unlimited development of mind and character. When at any age of life men and women begin to settle down, to stop learning and changing from within, they fall into the danger of ageing like the animals instead of living towards the future as human beings.

Experience of life can show that the child has to go through three stages of birth before he is fully grown. He has to be born three times over. At the first birth, the physical body separates from that of the mother. For a long while the little body cannot live and grow without adult help and care. Bit by bit the child learns to use the growing body and to reach new stages of independence. But the observer will be misled, if he imagines that the mind and soul are already independent. They are still carried in an invisible sheath, provided by the parents and the family. It is a big moment in the small child's life when he first says "no". He is preparing for a second separation which will only be accomplished much later. At the second birth, another part of the child's being separates itself from the mother. He will be by then about seven years old and will have started to replace the milk teeth by the second set. The life-body, which gives vitality to the physical, and forms the constitution, begins to become independent. The process again takes several years to complete. The child still needs the family very much during this period. He will be growing less like his parents and his brothers and sisters. He will be developing his own style of character and going his own path of experience at school and among his friends. But he needs the shelter of the family behind him. His soul is not yet strong enough to leave the soul-sheath in which his mother and father have protected him.

At the third birth childhood is left behind and youth begins. Behind the outer symptoms of puberty, the process is beginning to take place by which the soul throws off the last sheath and develops into an independent personality. The young person comes into his own. Turning inwards, he finds himself as a separate being with powers of thinking, feeling and willing to handle in his own way. Turning outwards, he faces the world, which grows bigger and more complicated before his gaze, the more he learns about it. Many a boy or girl encountering the shock of feeling him- or herself standing alone between the world within and the world without, longs to return to the shelter of childhood. But the deep urge of his or her own nature towards becoming grown-up pushes forward the process of separation despite the tendency to hang back. The dilemma is felt of going forward because it is impossible to turn back. The experience can be confusing for all concerned. The young person is alternately fascinated by the thrill of all that opens before him and repelled by anxieties and dread. The parents and older people are perplexed to know where to help and when to avoid interfering. All the wisdom of loving hearts is needed just at this time.

In a previous chapter, the process of being born and coming down to earth has been compared to a journey into the unknown. The picture can be carried further to describe the stage of youth. Birth, the great venture into earth-existence, starts the eternal soul off on the journey in a state of helplessness. The child cannot manage alone. But parents, teachers and other helpers are at hand to give the traveller a good start. It is their natural function to help while the condition of helplessness lasts but also to assist the child in becoming independent. The more and the better they help, the less they are needed and the more capable he becomes of travelling on alone. One day they come to the point of seeing him off, waving farewell as he sets out by himself, strong in the care and confidence they have given to him. They are parting from the child in the hope of receiving him back again as a grown-up person, who could become a life-long friend.

Will he bring it off? Will he make good? Will he arrive at his right destination? All who love him carry this question anxiously in their hearts and he is just as anxious as they. The young person cannot help knowing that he is facing a big test of himself as he travels forward into life. He is capable of every kind of misery, fear, despair, and the wish to run away and get back to childhood but also of every kind of enthusiasm, hope, self-confidence and the longing to rush on with life and conquer it. Most young people go through the whole range of such reactions and they behave as erratically as they feel. But underneath the changing pull of emotion they sense the fundamental question: "Shall I win through? Shall I make good? Shall I come rightly to the journey's end?"

This period of life, called youth for our present purpose, lasts in general about seven years, from fourteen to twenty-one. The process of parting from parents and teachers and setting out alone is slow and gradual. Every now and then, some event comes about that makes everyone aware of what is going on and remains as a milestone in the memory. But growing up is not over in a day and all the members of the family have a long period in which to adjust themselves to the changing situation. Pace becomes of first importance at this stage and it will often be the lot of the grown-up to watch over and regulate it. Each boy or girl needs his or her own pace of development. The one who rushes forward too fast and behaves too soon as a grown-up becomes a weak and inadequate adult, and the one who is a child too long becomes foolish and immature. The slow developer needs to be egged on and the quick one slowed down. But neither will be able to find the balance without grown-up help.

Very few people will be able to look back on this part of their lives without having to recall experiences of confusion, of painful emotion and of awkward behaviour. All these tended to produce an acute sense of being on one's own, facing great thoughts within and great trials without. Small events could produce such great shocks. A young girl at a party, who had recently been deeply affected by stories of famous martyrs, began to entertain her friends with her favourite ones. After a time the blank and bored look on their faces struck home to her. Not one of them is likely still to remember that moment but the girl of that day will never forget it. She realized for the first time what it can mean to be a bore, to address an uninterested audience, to be left alone with one's own great vision unshared. How comforting it was at this age of chilling self-awareness to be absorbed into a group, a team, a gang or a clique of friends, everyone acting alike, each if need be as silly as the others. But even that helped only for a while and back came the opposite urge towards one's own personality, towards being different, towards the search for one's own vision.

The need of the boy or girl for God goes through the same dramatic change as every other experience does at this age. The beginning of this period in life, that is to say the age of fourteen, should be marked by the act of Confirmation, to which reference has already been made. The inner impulse towards change in the soul of the growing boy or girl should be met and strengthened by a public act performed on behalf of the church or community to which the parents belong. Confirmation changes the status of the boy or girl in the religious community. Throughout childhood the ministers have taught and cared for him or for her, helping the teachers in their task of upbringing. Now, on behalf of all who have shared this responsibility, they solemnly dismiss the child from their authority and send him out into life. In the same religious act, they receive him as a young person into their fellowship and offer him the adult privilege of taking communion at the table of Christ. He is acknowledged as a fellow-worshipper with his own religious independence. Such is the custom in the Christian churches, and in other religions other rites of initiation into adult life are held at the same stage. The great danger is encountered in modern times, that the religious development of the young person comes to a stop here. Much popular religion today is on the level of a child's mind.

Ministers, parents and teachers take on a new responsibility towards the young people who have received their Confirmation. They should lead them into a grown-up religious life, showing them how to find a more inward relation to the world of God, just at the time when they are growing further into the world of the earth. When people travel abroad in a country where they have never been before, they are often glad to be shown round by a guide or courier and to hear what he has to tell. Older people who have information to offer and behave with tact, are very welcome to the young, and act as guides on the road of life.

A deep change within the young person's soul is the inner counterpart to the change of status in the religious community. He becomes intensely aware of what is within himself and belongs to him individually. He needs to find the working of God manifested in this experience. "God is within me, God is within the being of other people. It is a fact which I know of myself," so the heart of the young person speaks. The experience may be felt and expressed in many different ways. The core of the matter was once put into words by a young woman who had suffered a disfiguring illness in childhood and was writing the story of her early life. (*The Little Locksmith* by Katharine Butler Hathaway.) She described how it became clear to her one day that divine forces were at work within her and she began to go about with the shining thought, "God within me". With the help of this inner light, she began to overcome her fear of other people and of the world around her. She had made the most important discovery of youth.

The indwelling power of God discovers itself to the young soul in the shining visions, which are called ideals. "Youthful idealism" is a common expression which is used in many tones of voice. It can carry the cynical implication that the highflown emotions of a young person are not to be taken seriously. It can mean sympathy mixed with distrust. It should in reality be used with the greatest respect. To feel ideals strongly and clearly is the divine gift of youth, just as to be innocent is the gift of childhood. . . . If the gift is lost in later years, it is the tragic result of the failure to make the step forward in religion, which the young person needs.

Each of the three stages of birth is accompanied by a gift, of which the capacity for idealism is the last. Among the poets, Shelley has described it with the greatest force at the close of his poem: "Prometheus Unbound".

> "To suffer woes which hope thinks infinite;
>   To forgive wrongs darker than death or night;
>   To defy power which seems omnipotent;
>   To love and bear; to hope till hope creates
>   From its own wreck the thing it contemplates;
>   Neither to change, nor falter, nor repent;
>   This, like thy glory, Titan, is to be
>   Good, great and joyous, beautiful and free;
>   This is alone Life, Joy, Empire and Victory."

Is this romantic exaggeration? For the young soul in whom the forces of idealism are rising into consciousness, these are not highflown words. All that they say is so real and true that if the staider, older people around cannot appreciate them, the boy or girl begins to feel solitary and misunderstood. As a child he or she will have felt with awe the wisdom, greatness and goodness of God. Now the feeling arises: within my soul is carried a flame from the Divine Fire, that burns with the same light and strength within me as in the world. No ideal can be too high, no vision can be too great, no deed too heroic. However awkwardly expressed this feeling may be in the young person's talk or behaviour, it is still of the highest value. It is a sign that the soul is preparing itself for the grown-up knowledge of God.

The child knows God who is, in whose existence the world rests and evolves, the loving Father of us all. The grown-up should learn the mystery of the Son-God, of Him who is the creating Spirit of the world, and leads the evolution of Mankind towards its right, God-willed end. The Christian idea of the Trinity, of the Godhead in whom three beings work together as Father-god, Son-god and Spirit-god, arises from a fact of human experience, which is as true for those who do not acknowledge it in thought, as for those who are able to do so. . . . We are aware of God's working in three ways. We feel that our life is carried by and rests in the divine forces at work in the universe. Our feeling says: the Father-god is. We realize that a divine creative energy is working within each individual soul, which gives him his separate and unique value. Our feeling says: the Son-god is creating. We know that certain thoughts live in our hearts by which we are guided and inspired with faith. Our feeling says: the Spirit-god enlightens. Every human being who is awake to his humanity knows in himself the threefold working of divine forces, those that are, that create and that enlighten. Such an experience comes to grown-up people but not to children, because only the fully-grown person can be aware of the threefold activity of the Divine within him. The child can perceive the All-Father, the God from whom we all were born. The young person awakens to the divine power creating within his soul, when he feels the strength of his ideals. But he is not yet ready for the third revelation, for knowledge of the Spirit-god. That lies ahead, when the third birth is complete. He needs in the years of his youth to grow from knowledge of the Father-god into knowledge of the Son-god. He will not then fall into the danger of remaining a child in religious matters all his days. He will grow up in religion, until as a man he can acknowledge the threefold revelation of Father, Son and Spirit.

The Bible in its composition follows the path of experience, which is followed as the child becomes a youth. The Old Testament describes how God was experienced by Mankind in the childhood of the human race. The transition to the New Testament represents the change of experience at the beginning of youth. The Old Testament tells how the world was created by God, how man began his existence in the shadow of the Divine Presence. Mankind, originating with God, afterwards falling away into sin and separation, is its theme. Each growing child repeats it in his own experience. The New Testament tells how the Son of God came to earth and lived in human form for the sake of lost Mankind. Its theme is the descent into death and Christ's resurrection to life. The child sees the mystery of birth and learns to know the Father. The youth beholds the mystery of death that he may be able to realize the nature of the Son. To pass in thought from the

Old Testament to the New is to turn from Man's past to his future, to go from Mankind's childhood into the adult stage in evolution. The gaze which first beheld Man's beginning with God, looks towards his ending, when through Christ he is to take his appointed place in the spiritual universe as the Son resurrected from the death of earth existence. Will Mankind achieve the divine purpose? Will Man win through? The question that each young person asks for himself, when he faces his own future, is part of the great riddle of human evolution.

When the inner fires of the soul begin to waken and bring forth ideals, it is important for the spiritual health that they should become rightly connected with the needs of the world around. It is easy at this stage of growth for the soul to turn inwards and become self-absorbed, for the visions to be fantastic and the enthusiasm narrow. The divine forces within should stream towards the working of God outside in the world. The young person, who is finding himself, will need help towards discovering his part in history. It is a tragic thing when older people, looking back, can remember a religious phase passed through in youth and left behind when the cares of this world began to press hard. If the trend towards religion had been taken seriously at the time and older people had helped to give it a useful direction, this need not have happened. The counterbalance to the inner enthusiasm of youth is to understand history spiritually, that is to say, to see God at work there. The inner powers of the soul are not meant for oneself, they are one's individual offering to the progress of the world. Youth is the time for understanding one's place in world-history.

Man's spiritual evolution is following a certain trend. It began in the heights with Man emerging from the Gate of Heaven and took, at the temptation and fall, the downward direction. The line is one of continual descent until the coming to earth of the Son of God in Christ Jesus. From the time of His deed of death and life on the cross, a new line upwards has begun. Man has the opportunity to ascend again to the Father in the Heavens. But there is a choice. Human souls have in the past been pulled downwards on the descending line by a force of history. To join the ascent is an act of individual will which each must make for himself. There is a second historical trend, which can also be followed, the curve of continued descent away from the Heavens. No one can ascend only by the force of history, he must rise by his own free will. So it comes about that, although the entry of Christ into the world of earth has brought the decisive change into evolution, each person can only recognize the fact by his own insight. It is for himself to see or not to see.

Healthy children, given proper love and care, will be naturally religious, being aware of the Divine Presence of their own accord. Those who have left childhood behind, come to the point where they begin to have personal responsibility in their spiritual life. They become aware of the great question, the core of Man's whole evolution. What will become of Mankind? What shall become of ourselves? The natural faith of childhood cannot answer the riddle of the future. Spiritual faith created from within the individual soul is needed. Among the parables in the New Testament, one especially describes the great dilemma of Man's evolution, the story of the Prodigal Son. (St Luke, chapter 15.) It tells how the Father in the Heavens allows his younger son to leave home and start an independent existence in a far country. A rich inheritance is given him and he lives without work or care. But he is unable to appreciate the value of what he has received. He wastes his all in the company of greedy acquaintances. When his wealth is at an end, there is famine in the land. He is given a job as a pig-keeper, but what the pigs can eat, does not nourish him. In loneliness and want, he reaches the turning-point in his life. He comes to himself, and resolves to find the way back to the Father's house, to acknowledge his failure and ask for a servant's job. The way out from the Father's house was easy, but he has to go back alone by his own strength, knowing himself poor and unworthy. He returns and the Father welcomes him back, with particular joy, giving him the robe, the ring and the shoes of an honoured son. He welcomes him as no one ever before was welcomed, "for this my son was dead and is alive again, was lost and is found." When in the loneliness of earth-existence, a human soul comes to himself and sets out to find his way to the Father, he is taking the line of ascent to the World of the Spirit. He has made the decision for his own sake, but as he is not alone in the world, he is deciding as a member of Mankind. He is answering the question of Man's future in himself.

II

LEARNING RELIGION

"O WILD West Wind, Thou breath of Autumn's being" is the opening line of Shelley's ode to the Spirit in Nature. The young poet, feeling forces of soul surging within himself, seeks the companionship of another being of like mood, urged on by an impulse akin to his own and finds it in the wind that presides over the fall of the year. Shelley addresses the wind as a companion, a living Spirit with whom he can talk. In a similar mood, meteorologists, whose job it is to measure the force and chart the direction of winds, are known to give girls' names to the storms whose course they track. They may put it into more ordinary terms but they also are perceiving the "unseen presence" to whom Shelley speaks:

> "Wild Spirit which art moving everywhere,
> Destroyer and preserver, hear oh hear."

The poem becomes a prayer to the companion Spirit of the wind.

> "Make me thy lyre, even as the forest is:
> What if my leaves are falling like its own?
> The tumult of thy mighty harmonies
> Will take from both a deep autumnal tone,
> Sweet though in sadness. Be thou, Spirit fierce,
> My spirit! Be thou me, impetuous one!
> Drive my dead thoughts over the universe
> Like withered leaves, to quicken a new birth."

Such a thought is naturally and easily understood during the years of youth. A child can be very happy out of doors, looking for favourite flowers at the different seasons, striking up heartfelt friendships with animals and birds. If he has rightly learnt lessons in religion, he will associate what he observes with his thoughts about the wisdom of God. His holier feelings will flow into what he thinks and how he behaves towards all living creatures. A young person can feel just as strong an urge to get out into Nature but with his growing strength of limb, it will take a different form. He will want wide horizons, distant landscapes, high mountains and broad rivers. Instead of the child's fondness for things little and near, he will long for what is far off and unknown. He will tend to feel like Shelley the longing to find echoed back to him from Nature the powerful surge of feeling that rises up in his own growing soul. In a modern young person, a particular kind of tension may often make itself felt at this age. At school he will learn the so-called scientific outlook on the world, in which that will seem real which can be explained in material and mechanical terms. In his spare time he will want to get away into the countryside and feel in his heart a conversation between his spirit and the unseen presence in wind and water, earth and sky, like Shelley's prayer in poetry to the West Wind. Can he ever hope to reconcile the two?

His religious life can present a great problem to the growing mind of a young person. He cannot be properly irreligious, as a grown-up person can become, because his fresh forces of feeling make him sensitive to the unseen presences that older people can more easily ignore. But the thoughts in which he is educated do not meet his experience and he may be driven to lead a double life, one imaginative, emotional and religious, the other intellectual, clever and scientific. This can only make him into a divided character, too fantastic on the one hand and too hard-headed on the other. If the boy or girl is rightly to learn religion in his young years for the sake of the grown-up person he is becoming, he will need to be taught how to bridge the gap. A bridge can be found when appreciation is developed for the reality that spiritual facts are just as real and factual as material ones. The two types of fact may have to be looked at side by side. One might say, Shelley's West Wind had a gale force that could be measured and the leaves that fled before it "yellow and black and pale and hectic red, pestilence-stricken multitudes" were undergoing changes in chemical composition. That is one kind of fact and the other of equal reality is that with which the poem closes:

"The trumpet of a prophecy! O Wind,
    If Winter comes, can Spring be far behind?"

If both can be accepted as facts, religion and science stand side by side and the mind of the young person need not be divided between opposites.

The upsurge of natural religious feeling, which is common in the teenage, can become "just one of those phases" to be outgrown. Equally it can be the opportunity for planting in the heart the religious life that will reach its flowering in grown-up years. The best condition for cultivating the seed in youth will be given when young people come in contact with older ones, whose outlook has developed a stage further than that which has just been described. Spiritual and material facts may be accepted on the same level of reality but still more is achieved, if an inner relation between them is discovered. That will mean to comprehend how spirit becomes matter and matter returns to spirit. A long line of spiritually-minded thinkers, including such great figures as Goethe, culminated in this century in Rudolf Steiner who called his way of thinking "spiritual science". He brings about as a natural development the reconciliation of science, art and religion, not in theory, but in reality. An important consequence arises, of value to everyone, however little philosophically inclined he may be. The cleft between the three has caused the minds of modern people to be split up into separate departments. Clear thinking in a whole mind has become increasingly difficult to achieve, with the result that many people continually contradict themselves in their own thoughts without realizing what they are doing. Such a contradiction is to be seen in the split between faith and knowledge, which is a dogma in one Christian Church. That knowledge reaches as far as a frontier which cannot be crossed, while faith begins on the far side and the two can never meet, is the teaching upheld. Equally contradictory is the type of religious thought by which it is admitted that our souls inhabit material bodies on earth, but matter is denied except as a sinful delusion. Such beliefs have the effect of confusing the minds of those who hold them and endangering the wholeness of their personalities.

It is of the greatest value to the spiritual health of young people to be saved from the disintegrating influence of a divided outlook on the world in the years during which the religious life is being formed for the future. Instead of becoming split personalities of the kind so common nowadays, they can hope to become whole people in whose life of the mind religion has a natural place at the centre. Religion should not be a set of beliefs, which have been taught to the young people, and to which, in the form of a creed, they are asked to subscribe. Doctrine is always a second best for living experience to awaken and cultivate which is the true aim of religious instruction. Take the following example by way of illustration. Man is made in the image of God. Such a statement, founded on what is said in the Bible, can be made a point of doctrine. But the idea may become a living experience if a certain outlook is cultivated. One can say to one's self: how can I know what a rose is? The full-blown rose shows me only one stage in a process, which continues through the four seasons of the year. Can I call one passing appearance "the rose" and not the other? I can know the one by following its existence through the course of the year from budding to blossoming, fading and lying dormant until the next quickening.

Likewise, to learn what Man is, I must see him in time, watching how a human being passes through the stages of a lifetime. The baby, the child, the youth, the man or woman, the person in middle life, the same one in old age are all manifestations of the being "Man". Beyond the two thresholds of birth and death another part of man's being is glimpsed. There he is with God, here he reflects His image. In the whole cycle of a human being's moving existence the true picture of Man can be found. Every person we meet, ourselves included, is on the move from birth towards death and towards the other half of existence beyond the barrier. We cannot know what we are capable of, what forces are hidden in our nature, if we only see ourselves in one of life's moments. Each person's biography reflects the image of God in him. Our feeling for what is divine, our reverence for it is nourished when we are made aware of what grows, lives and changes in life. We become more religious people in proportion as we have an eye for what develops from one stage to another, for what quickens, fades, disappears, and returns in a higher form.

We get to know the human being by following him through the changing phases of a lifetime and Mankind through the changing course of world history. Religion should be taught to young people through history in the first place. They should be shown the broad picture in which all faiths are included, and each particular one finds its place. The years of youth are not the occasion for reaching decisions about beliefs, making up one's mind to accept one religion or another, or to join a church. The young person should first "shake hands with time" as a Jacobean poet once said. He should learn something of Mankind's past, then he will have the means in later years of estimating the different faiths known at the present time. Some parents hold the view that by rearing their growing children without any guidance on religion, they are "leaving them free to make their own decisions". In fact, they are all too often leaving them confused and uncertain, because they have no inner means of making such a decision. It is equally unhelpful if the opposite line is taken and parents teach that only one religion or one church is right and all others are wrong and dangerous. Young people should be given the means of developing a sense of direction in religious matters, so that later on they can have an independent judgement. In a wide, meaningful view of history, they will learn what they need. Instead of encountering the rights and wrongs of various creeds, they will first get to know Mankind by "shaking hands with time".

It has already been said in an earlier chapter that the pattern of Man's evolution is outlined in the Bible and is repeated in the experience of the growing child. The young person will need to learn about the historical material, which fills in the outline. The first half of history should be the line of Man's descent from the Divine World, from which he originated, to independent existence in the world of earth. It was the force of Evil which pushed Man on the downward path. At the beginning of history, he was exposed to temptation, Evil was allowed to attack him and he, the being who had been entirely sheltered in the presence of God, was driven out into a world that had begun to separate itself off from the Divine. A long historical process began which plunged human souls, in the life between birth and death, further and further into the fallen state where they were continually exposed to the temptations of Evil. Religion became the means of keeping contact with the divine world of their origin and was inspired by the longing to come close again to God. It expressed the homesickness of the soul for its spiritual home and the regret fot its original innocence. Religions of the ancient world directed her gaze back through time to the beginning of existence.

All early religions had this common origin and impulse, but they were not otherwise the same. The peoples of the world were divided into nations, races and tribes all with their own kinds of religion. Human beings were born into families and tribes which were likewise religious communities. Each tribe had a genius or a god who inspired his people with divine guidance of a particular kind. It was wrong in those times for a person to desert the "god of his fathers" and follow the god of another tribe. Many and varied were the divine beings who inspired the different people of the world. But behind them, concealed in the mystery of His greatness, the presence was felt of "the God of gods", the one Father of all, who spoke through His divine representatives to His children. No one people alone could comprehend the whole being of God but He was manifested in many forms in different parts of the earth. The picture of God was spread out over the whole world, each tribe or nation being entrusted with its particular portion. The spiritual treasures of all the nations together made up the whole. No religion was right and the other wrong, but each was necessary to the others.

As the descent of Man continued from age to age, the tragedy of Man's life on earth increased. The religions of all the peoples became weaker and less able to bring God nearer to Mankind. Human hearts darkened, wrongdoing increased and in their independence from the Divine, men fell more and more under the influence of Evil. History became a world-dilemma, for which there was no solution on earth. In all the different religions of the world at that time, a common inspiration began to appear. It was expected everywhere that a Saviour would come to solve the dilemma, and that He would be, not a man but a god, and not one of the tribal gods, but the Son of God Himself. The Jewish people, whose history is described in the Old Testament, were devoted as a nation to preparing the way for the coming of the Messiah. They felt themselves to be a people chosen for this purpose beyond all others, and they had a particular right to this conviction. Theirs was the task of preparing through many generations the physical body, into which the descending God would enter. In this respect they were chosen by the Divine Will, but the expectation of a great coming from the World of God was shared after their own fashion by all the peoples of that time.

In the pattern of Mankind's history each of the religions that lived among the peoples of the world during the time of Man's descent was a right part of God's revelation on earth. Each of them prepared the way for the coming of the Son of God, Christ, to overcome the dilemma into which Mankind had fallen. The great teachers of the ancient world were His prophets as much as those of the Jewish people, known to us from the Old Testament. Nowdays many people know the teachings of Mankind's great leaders, of Confucius, of Buddha, and many more. Their true greatness is seen when their place is realized in the perspective of time. Each young person needs to learn something of comparative religion from this point of view.

The coming of Christ to earth is the turning-point of Mankind's evolution. He performed on the Cross the divine deed, in which death was overcome and the life of the Resurrection was born. The descent of Man is transformed into ascent by the power streaming into evolution from the creative act of Christ's Resurrection. A new impulse of Spirit entered history and whereas the old religions were inspired by the longing to look back to the beginning of Man's existence, modern religion should be filled with the urge to look forward. The idea of Resurrection should be the chief inspiration in our minds today. The poet Shelley felt this thought stirring within him, when he finished his "Ode to the West Wind" with the words: "If Winter comes, can Spring be far behind?" A few lines before he had written, "drive my dead thoughts over the universe," feeling in his own soul the infection of death, by which all Mankind had been caught. Aware of death, he looked for the promise of life. What is to come must be life, must be renewal, if Man is to continue his history.

Shelley has called the last words of the Ode "the trumpet of a prophecy", that is to say, a reality still to come in the future. He was expressing his longing to find the power of Resurrection but it was beyond his reach. The Spring comes again through the earth's power to renew life. Renewal brings a foretaste of Resurrection but not its essence. The Spring can give new life to Nature and to Man in so far as he depends on Nature. But it cannot change the descending line of Man's evolution into ascent. A new impulse of creative power from the source of all creation in the Spiritual World itself is the essence of resurrection. The Son of God, sacrificing His own being into the coming evolution of Mankind, makes Himself into the living ladder between earth and Heaven on which Man can ascend. Jacob, one of the heroes of the Old Testament, once had a prophetic dream in which he saw a golden ladder set up between earth and Heaven, on which angels went up and down. When Christ had overcome death on the Cross and risen again, the prophetic dream had become a fact. His spirit-being is the ladder on which human souls find the way upwards to the Worlds of Spirit. St Paul concentrated in one short sentence the mystery of Resurrection, when he declared: "If Christ be not risen, your faith is in vain."

Christianity is not one religion among many others. The coming of the Son of God, for whom the title "Christ" is used, is a fact of world-history and the turning-point of Man's evolution. Christ has brought the power of Resurrection into Man's life on the earth, solving the world dilemma, through which history was once in danger of coming to a standstill. Evolution is again in motion, but now with a double trend, one upwards on the line of Man's ascent, the other downwards in the direction of the world's end. Christianity, in this sense, means understanding the spiritual fact at the core of evolution. Young people will have the best introduction to religion if they learn to see the picture of world-history in its widest expanse, from beginning to end. They will find themselves learning to know Christ, not as the founder of a new religion, but as the divine Saviour of Mankind from the dilemma brought about by evolution. They will face the question: how can I understand what has happened in the past, what now is, and what should come in the future?

In the past, it was necessary that as many religions existed on earth as there were peoples, led and inspired by different divine beings representing one part of the whole being of God. Since the coming of Christ, religious life has come to depend, not on tribe and nation, but on the individual soul. There are as many religions now as there are people aware of the Divine Spirit within themselves. Each person has his own religion and when he experiences the power of Resurrection within himself, he is recognizing Christianity. Does this mean the end of all organized religion? What do the many religious bodies mean, the many kinds of Christian church mean, which we encounter and the young people will meet as they go out into the world? Time has been compared to "an ever-rolling stream". It bears us all onwards through history but it carries on its waters many kinds of craft that started their journey at earlier points on its course. All were up-to-date at one stage but some are quite out-of-date now. Some churches or religious bodies are loved by their adherents just because they are in an old style and belong to the past. The religious community of a truly modern kind is still in the process of being constructed. It will rest on the principle, which sounds to be a contradiction but in fact is not, that each person now finds his religion within himself but, if he is to thrive in soul, needs to join in a spiritual community with other people.

Young people learning religion through world history should get to know as much as possible of the great teachings of the past that are left to us in written form. They should not just know the great teachers by name and reputation but should become their pupils by listening to their thoughts. The more experience can be absorbed in the years of youth the better. It is no matter if much is not yet understood. In the busy grown-up years there will be less time and strength for reading and exploring but memories will return of thoughts half-understood before and then seen more clearly. To listen in youth to Buddha preaching to his followers, to Isaiah addressing his hearers, Socrates questioning his pupils, to name only three of the many to be heard, enriches the mind for life. Most of all in those years, the four Gospels should become familiar reading. They may be studied in class at school or in church very usefully, but in the first place they belong to the personal religious life. They are the portrait of Christ at the time when He lived on the earth, when He walked with men and women, teaching, healing and working as the Son of God who had made Himself Son of Man. Pondering over the words of the Gospels, we become disciples ourselves and hear them again as they live today. "We shake hands with time" and find that we have touched the everlasting.

III

PRAYER

THE child's first prayer is said, before he can speak, by his mother and father on his behalf. One day he is able to say the words with them. Later on he wishes to say the prayer by himself, while they listen. But there comes the time when he leaves childhood behind and wants the privacy to pray by himself and use prayers that he has accepted on his own account. In every respect his relationship to his parents will be changing at this time but the matter of prayer will often bring the change abruptly to notice. Sometimes the parents do not accept the withdrawal into privacy happily, but sometimes the child is reluctant, when the parents would like to encourage the step. No real difficulty will arise, when the older people are sufficiently confident on spiritual matters to talk them over in a calm, impersonal way with the boy or girl who is growing up. If they can show him a grown-up person can pray, they will be offering a guiding thought to the boy or girl, who is being left on his or her own. The grown-ups should be able to speak impersonally while realizing that no one passing through his or her teens can be expected to do so. Too many grown-ups today have never properly outgrown the emotional confusion of their own adolescence. In reality, the distinction between a grown-up and a young person lies in this, that the latter cannot avoid being involved with his personal emotions in everything, while the former should be able to attain detachment.

It has been suggested in the previous chapter that young people should learn to absorb the course of world-history. Their intellectual forces are unfolding at this age and they benefit from the effort to turn their interest away from themselves to the world. Nevertheless in this period of life, they are certainly made aware of the forces rising up within themselves. They are developing a conscious inner life, which cannot be ignored. They will need help in getting accustomed to it and in bringing it under their own direction. A person looking in upon himself encounters first of all a dilemma. He feels the contrast between the strength of his spiritual forces and the changeability of his thoughts and emotions. The poet Shelley has written a "Hymn to Intellectual Beauty" in which he expresses the inner dilemma of the soul:

> "The awful shadow of some unseen power
> Floats, though unseen, among us, visiting
> This various world with as inconstant wing
> As summer winds that creep from flower to flower.
> Like moonbeams that behind some piney mountain shower,
> It visits with inconstant glance
> Each human heart and countenance."

The spiritual power is felt within the soul, but it appears to withdraw again behind the changing emotions. How can the soul achieve any certainty within itself?

There was once a small boy with a loud voice, much given by temperament to shouting and howling. No requests to be quiet had any effect. One day in the midst of an outburst, he stopped dead and said in mild tones: "What am I making all this noise for?" In the years of adolescence the noise stops being physical and becomes psychological. It disturbs just as much but in a different way. The moment of saving grace comes when the girl or boy can pause and say to himself; what is all this noise for? In childhood dressing up is a favourite game. The clothes of the grown-ups, any piece of stuff to be laid hands on, will be worn so that the children can play one part after another. Some are clever enough to change their behaviour with each costume and to feel themselves becoming one character after another. In adolescence the game is repeated in a psychological way. A young person will imitate the opinions, the behaviour, the outlook and the manners of one character after another. If someone whom he encounters makes an impression on him, he will become a little copy of him for a while. Parents go through many alarms at this period, if they take too seriously these fashions of behaviour. The son or daughter is dressing up, to find out what it feels like to be different kinds of people. He or she feels inwardly obliged to be very serious about each character, for otherwise nothing would be learnt. But the older people can take a longer view and, if they have the right tact, help themselves with humour.

Whatever anxiety the older people may feel, they share it in reality with the youngsters. The game of psychological dressing-up must be played but it leaves the soul in a painful inner uncertainty. The young person has a great need of finding these moments of saving grace in which he realizes that at the core of his being there is a spiritual self on which he can rely because it is related to the Divine Spirit of the World, to God Himself. He is not in truth identified with all the changing thoughts and emotions which he experiences. In the moments when he is capable of realizing that this is so, his mind perceives the deep mystery of human existence, the contrast between what is mortal in us and what is immortal. He stands in spirit at the place where time and eternity meet. Shelley in his poem "Hymn" describes this experience as it came to him in his own youth. He perceived the immortal quality within himself and named it "Intellectual Beauty". He addressed it as a being, a goddess visiting his soul, to whom he can say "thou".

> "Love, Hope and Self-esteem, like clouds depart
> And come, for some uncertain moments lent.
> Man were immortal and omnipotent,
> Didst thou, unknown and awful as thou art,
> Keep with thy glorious train firm state within his heart."

He recalls the hour of experience, in which the realization came to him that an immortal presence can live in the changing life of a human soul.

> "Sudden thy shadow fell on me
>
> . . . .
> I vowed that I would dedicate my powers
> To thee and thine: have I not kept the vow?
>
> . . . .
> They know that never joy illumed my brow,
> Unlinked with hope that thou wouldest free

130

This world from its dark slavery:
That thou, O awful Loveliness,
Wouldst give whate'er these words cannot express."

The contrast between the immortal and the mortal in one's own soul and in the world is the deepest experience in the years of youth. It is beyond the understanding of most young people at the time when they encounter it. Shelley himself wrote the "Hymn" in later years, looking back on the crisis of his early youth. But whatever the degree of awareness may be, with which it is encountered by one young person or the other, it rouses in the depths of the heart the wish to pray. There is helplessness in having an experience which one cannot yet understand but which one can feel intensely. In this mood the soul turns to the divine source of all that is immortal in itself. "My immortal being recognizes the Immortal Being in the world" so the thought rises in the heart; "May the Immortal Being Divine look upon and protect the immortal being in me, which is in danger of being consumed by what is mortal." In some such words as these one might dare to express the unspoken thought which urges the young soul to pray.

Children pray differently from grown-ups. The time will now come when the boy or girl needs to learn all over again how to pray. It is not enough for parents or teachers to give him or her privacy in his or her religious life. Help and guidance on how to proceed at this new stage will be needed. Rightly speaking there is both public and private prayer to be thought of. Occasions for prayer in family life have already been described. Customs suitable for the children since they were small will have been long established. When the eldest one reaches the years of youth, a new element will be required without disturbing what still suits the younger ones. The grown-ups can explain that up to now, they have adjusted themselves for the most part to the needs of the children. But one of them is becoming a grown-up, so altering the balance within the family. More grown-up customs than formerly will now be followed, so that each group has its requirements. When, for instance, grace is said at a meal, where the whole family is assembled, one of the children will say the prayer, perhaps the youngest. But a second grace can be said by one of the grown-ups, a different one with more thought in it than the child's. Similarly, at a family gathering on a Sunday evening or other special occasion, what is read and sung will take on a new scope to include the taste and needs of the older members. It would be a mistake to ask the older ones to accept only verses, songs and readings which are taken for the sake of the younger ones. To do this soon has the effect of making religion into an affair of childhood, something to be outgrown.

At school and in church the transition is more easily made than at home. Boys and girls move up the school in age-groups and the teachers can introduce new customs at each stage. Here, as in the family, the problem of behaviour is the greatest hindrance. Children are more spontaneous in the way they behave than boys and girls who have reached the age of acute, embarrassing self-consciousness. Many older people feel the embarrassment so acutely that they begin to share it, instead of meeting it with detachment. The boys and girls are waiting for an older, more experienced person to make it possible for them to behave well. Prayer touches the deepest and most inward feeling of the heart and therefore becomes most easily involved with the embarrassment natural in youth. Any note of false piety, of forced emotion, is noticed and resented at once. Just because young people are forced by their own nature to feel everything in a personal and intense way, they need to meet what is spiritual, in this instance prayer, brought to them with objective detachment. They will protect themselves against appeals to their feeling from outside by putting on a hard shell. The custom of prayer will be continued in the school life right up to the top age-group without disturbance, if the teachers find the changes of style suited to each stage of development.

In church the matter takes on another aspect. The act of Confirmation, or that which corresponds to it, marks the dividing line between childhood and youth. The young people belong to the adult community and share in their services. But a gap is there to be bridged between their inner capacities and the outer experience. The Communion Service, for instance, represents something beyond them into which they have still to grow. How, at this stage, can help be given by older people without inter-ference? Young people enjoy getting together on their own. The strain of going through adolescence is eased for a while by each other's company. But they do not benefit by always being together because they are in fact busily learning to be grown-up and require older people from whom they can learn. The com-munity of the church should offer to people of all ages the opportunity to meet in common spiritual interests and so to develop relationships of a different kind from those outside. Young people spend considerable time together in school and college, in clubs and camps. If this pattern is simply repeated in the life of the church, they miss the opportunity to exchange thoughts with people more mature than themselves. Spiritually speaking, we all grow by looking beyond what we are already. Little children imitate, older ones worship heroes and young people, stirred by their feeling for ideals, want to know people who represent ideals in active life. They want, one might say, to learn how it is done, to keep ideals into the later years and make them real in experience. Such a need should be met in the life of the church.

Young people will want to hear from the older ones most of all how their private prayer can change as they themselves develop inwardly. Naturally, new forms of words should be found for them and the prayers of childhood laid aside. But apart from this practical aspect, the deeper side of the matter will need to be faced. The problem is fundamentally this: What is the need of prayer in youth and in grown-up life? The child needs to pray because he is still connected with the Divine World from which he has come and he seeks the working of God in the very different world of earth which he has just entered. The grown-up needs to pray because, in the course of growing up, he has discovered that he is a twofold being, with an immortal part living side by side with the mortal in his human nature. The mortal part has had to learn to deal with the mortal affairs of his existence. The immortal part can learn to pray because it is related to what is immortal in the universe, to the Divine World of Spirit. Youth is the time of life when each person discovers the contrast between what is mortal and what is immortal within himself, and feels the urge to pray just as truly as he feels urged to learn skill in handling the things of the world outside. If he is to become a complete and whole human being, he will have to hold the balance between outer and inner, mortal and immortal.

The immortal part in the soul is the one within who can pray. How does he speak, what can he say? The original pattern of prayer in Christian times is that given by Jesus Christ to His followers and known by old custom as the Lord's Prayer. No prayer has been repeated more often since Christianity began, and for some people it has grown stale for this very reason. But each young person should make his own acquaintance with it, not only as a prayer often said on public occasions, but as one to be said personally for himself. He will be starting afresh on the most familiar form of words that there is. Many other prayers can be said and will be discovered in the course of a lifetime. But the Lord's Prayer is the pattern, by which others can be measured for their value, and for this reason should be known as soon as the age for praying as a grown-up has come. Good taste is needed in spiritual things, and in order to develop it, the best pattern is required at the start. There is no space here for reviewing the many possible forms of prayer which can be used. The Lord's Prayer will therefore be taken now as the most valuable example, through which to illustrate some thoughts on the nature of prayer as such.

Will most young people not have already known this prayer as children? It is certainly very likely that they will have done so but even though they may have joined in repeating it, they will not have been able to pray it in the true sense. Children do not experience themselves or the Divine in such a way as to be able to use it as an individual prayer. There is much more to praying than repeating a form of words. This is part of the paradox that lies in the nature of prayer. On the one hand, the form of words used is often the same for long periods. Those who are skilled in prayer are they who change the words least frequently, because they have experienced that prayer becomes deeper and fuller the more it is truly prayed. In this sense repetition is a real part of praying. But as old as the words of Jesus to His Hearers revealed in the Gospels is the warning against vain, or empty, repetition.

For, on the other hand, to say a prayer is a fresh creative effort each time. To use the same words as before is not to save oneself making this effort. It can even be that to take a new form of words is usefully stimulating. But to take the same one again has nevertheless a particular value. A certain strength remains over from the effort made before and from the time before that. The process of deepening the experience is helped. The force of continuity makes itself felt. A parallel experience can be found in another kind of activity. Rowing or paddling a boat also means repeating the same effort over and over again. The necessary skill consists in the right handling of repetition. If the oar or the paddle is dipped in the water again too soon, the forward movement of the boat is hindered. If the next stroke is made too late, no way is left for use from the previous one. But if the motion of rowing or paddling is repeated with good timing the forward movement is carried on from one stroke to the next, that is to say, here is repetition at its most useful.

Prayer requires preparation, especially inner and outer quiet. A young person needs a certain portion of time and place for himself. Circumstances may make this hard to provide, but if the older people around realize the need to be a serious one, the means will usually be found. Outer quiet does not produce inner stillness of its own accord. The one who prays has to quieten his thoughts and concentrate them on the Being to whom the prayer is addressed. Prayer is as much listening as speaking. The first act of listening is to contemplate the picture of Him to whom the words are said. At the opening of the Lord's Prayer, the thoughts turn to the immortal Father of us all. Before the words, "Our Father", can be said, the thought must be present of the immortal part in myself, who can in truth say to God "Father". But the first word of address is not "my" but "our". The thought of the immortal part within my neighbour, within all those whom I love, all those whom I know without loving them and in an ever widening circle of those fellow-men of mine of whom I have only heard, or scarcely even that, should come alive. The word "Mankind" should awaken in my heart from its customary abstract meaning to the living picture of the great family of all who are human and who can all say with equal right "Our Father".

"The Father in the Heavens" is the second part of the picture. The earth is the mother of all in us that is mortal. In the Heavens dwells the Father of our immortal part, to whom we shall return, when the mortal is put off. Whatever claims our earth-existence makes upon us, we restore the balance in times of prayer by turning to the World where our immortal part belongs. When we speak in serious thought the opening words of the Lord's Prayer, we hear in answer the confirmation that in our true immortal being we belong to God and are His children. The first three petitions that follow this opening are to request that we shall remain during our earthly life united with Him, so living that His being may be revealed in and through us. "Hallowed be Thy name". The name of God on earth is that part of His being which we can recognize in our thoughts. We know Him by His name in our thinking. "Thy kingdom come." We feel the working of God with all our feelings that are sensitive to the Divine. Our hearts distinguish what is not divine from what is god-willed in the world around us. We pray that in us His kingdom may be extended on earth. "Thy will be done." May our actions be willed in God's will. May the world-purposes that live in the Heavens be active on earth in and through our human deeds. We pray to the Father in the Heavens that we His children may live as immortal beings in the mortal world of the earth.

Four petitions follow the first three in the Lord's Prayer, making seven in all. We pray in the first three that our immortal being may work within the Being of the Father during our mortal life. In the second four we pray that our mortal life on earth may be taken into the hands of the Father. We ask that it may be touched by His immortal power, that our immortal part may not be lost and swallowed up by mortality. "Give us this day our daily bread." May we receive what our bodies require, by which we are subject to the pressure of hunger and cold and through them to the power of money, in co-operation with the Divine World, through whom the earth was created. "Forgive us our trespasses." May we be healed of all that we have done out of the urges of fear and greed, that we may give healing to those who are guilty towards us. "Lead us not into temptation." May we be led through earth-existence, where we are separated from the Divine

World and exposed to the attacks of evil powers, by the voice of God speaking within our hearts, that the experiences of this world may not become temptations to us. "Deliver us from Evil." May the power of Evil be hindered from seizing on our immortal being, while we walk under its shadow through our earthly life. The last sentence of the prayer, which follows the seven petitions, is not recorded in the Gospel. It has arisen out of the hearts of those who repeated it in the first Christian centuries. They were acknowledging the working of God through the world.

If each of the petitions besides being said, is listened to, the answer to the prayer is heard in the praying. In the previous chapter, it was said that when the course of Man's evolution is understood, the idea of Resurrection will be seen to be the chief historical impulse of the present and the future. That which can be read in world-history is to be felt at work within each human heart. The immortal being in us dies into the mortal as we pass from childhood to grown-up life. But when that which is immortal within us prays to the immortal Father, the process of Resurrection begins. The Spirit of Christ is with us and within us throughout our life on earth. He is the immortal Brother, who watches over the immortal spirits within human hearts. He leads us towards the Father in the Heavens. Our mortal life is, in the words of Shelley, "an unquiet dream". The grace is His living presence here on earth and the truth is the Resurrection, the rising again of Man who passes through mortality into immortality. When here on earth, turning to the Heavens, we say, "Our Father", we feel that the immortal spirit speaks in us, we are aware that Christ is with us. So we pray, speaking and listening, asking and receiving.

IV

CONSCIENCE

A SMALL boy came home from school one day and said to his mother: "There is a boy in my school who doesn't believe in God. His father says he doesn't believe in God. Isn't it sad? I'm so sorry for him." Protected at home by the warm religious feeling of his parents, the boy could face the early shocks of experience outside with well-rooted confidence. His first encounter with unbelief made him, not fearful, but sad. In childhood the final word in every question is usually "my mother says", "my father thinks" or "the teacher said at school". Adolescence means the end of unquestioning reliance on the judgement of older people. The need to make one's own standards, to find out by one's own experience, begins to make itself felt. The shelter of authority has to be left behind and the venture made into uncertainty. Some boys and girls go through a spell of opposition and defiance at this age. A certain element of protest against the behaviour of the grown-ups prompts this reaction, for which the older people might justly have to share the blame. The critical faculties have woken up and the young person can compare the idealized picture he saw in the people round him as a child with the unsatisfactory figures they cut for him now. It is painful for all concerned and the young person becomes oversensitive to any discrepancy between what the older ones set out to be and the way in which they behave. At this point in the history of the family, those parents do best, who have never demanded more love and respect than the children could offer spontaneously.

The child will have been brought up in certain habits and by certain standards. They will all come under question for the young person, because he needs to find his own relationship to them. If the older people are active enough in mind, they will enter into the questioning in a friendly way, not to defend their standards but to see them in a fresh light. Companionship between older and younger people is very fruitful at this age but there are two natural hindrances to its development. The one is inertia on the part of the older ones. Young children want the grown-ups to play with them, but adolescents want them to explore life with them. Mental inertia or mental cowardice become the gravest sins. The other is uncertainty on the part of the young people. They do not know their way about life. They can be so easily misled or disappointed. They must be convinced that confidence in any particular grown-up will not be misplaced or misused. Older people have to imagine the confusion which struggles with hope in the young soul. Younger ones need to learn how to appreciate the strains and stresses to which the older ones have been exposed. With effort on both sides, the companionship may be established and bring real blessing, the younger ones growing less foolish and the older ones less stuck in their ways.

Life is full of contradictions, which the young person does not know how to solve. As a child he was told fairy stories and recognized the simple opposites, the good and beautiful princess and the jealous stepmother, the generous fairy-godmother and the ugly witch. As an adolescent, he finds more complicated contradictions in himself, and in his experiences with the world. Shelley spoke of the inner mood of the soul like this:

"We look before and after
And pine for what is not.
Our sincerest laughter
With some pain is fraught.
Our sweetest songs are those that tell of saddest thought."

The years of youth bring the joy of going to meet life in the glow of ideals, that seem as if they could never be lost or forgotten. Enthusiasm burns brightly in the strong young heart and can revive the flame in the weary hearts of older people. But there is a shadow to the joy. The sense of sin is very much awake at the time in life when the ideals shine most clearly. In childhood the fall of Man comes to be accepted as a fact of existence. In youth it is felt more inwardly and personally. The terrifying shadow of his own capacity for wickedness falls across the hope with which the young person faces the venture of life. The tragedy in our earth-existence becomes clear and near. Once again, it should be stressed at this point that such experiences may take on the most varied forms, because every human being is individual and different. Nevertheless there is a trend of experience, known alike to everyone, running through the process of growing-up.

Three schoolgirls, soon to leave school, were out walking once with a grown-up. They were discussing the problems of life earnestly, but in the grand manner, which is so sure a sign of inexperience. They were healthy and as happy as healthy natures could make them. Every problem they touched on was made a matter of right and wrong, of better and worse. At last the grown-up asked whether they thought that people whose lives were unhappy would be morally better than those whose lives were happy. With one accord they pronounced that unhappiness improved people's characters and was good for them. They had no doubts about it and when the grown-up told of happy people she had known, who had shed sunshine upon all around them, they looked dubiously at her, as at someone with low standards. The tendency towards moralizing arises among adolescents from their inner feeling for the conflict between their capacity to believe in ideals and the tendency to fall into sin. They are preoccupied with the contradictions in their own human nature. In later years they may settle down to expect little of themselves, but not in youth. The sense of sin, which may fall asleep in older people, is wide awake. The behaviour of adolescents can be very deceptive and their opinions may be deplorable but more often than not they are putting on a show, or making experiments. It does them wrong not to see through the appearance to the deeper reality, to their longing that the good in them shall overcome their evil. Only in young people whose whole constitution is unhealthy will the moral sense be missing.

"For the good that I would I do not, but the evil which I would not, that I do." So St Paul, writing to the Christians in Rome, described the dilemma in which the human being finds himself here on earth. We recognize it as St Paul did by the inner sight given to us by the conscience. At the time in history before each separate person had his own inner sense of right and wrong, the authority of the Law prevailed. The change came when Christ appeared on earth. The Sermon on the Mount, recorded in St Matthew's Gospel, described the contrast between the old law given to Moses by Jehovah and the new teaching of Christ. "It hath been said" is the phrase indicating the old Law. It is followed by another, "But I say unto you", introducing the new principle. The contrast between the old and the new, which lies in the small word "but", is between outer and inner, between behaviour and motive. One example begins: "It was said 'Thou shalt not kill'. But I say unto you, Whosoever is angry with his brother without a cause shall be in danger of the judgement." Another runs: "It hath been said 'An eye for an eye, and a tooth for a tooth': But I say unto you, that you resist not evil." So through a long passage in the Sermon, the contrast is drawn between the actions condemned of old in the Law and the impulses of the heart stressed in the teaching of Christ. According to the old way, behaviour which did not offend against the Law was good. But by the new principle the motive in the heart is judged by the conscience, which sees the thought within before the action outside.

In the course of history the authority of the Law was first given to Mankind to keep them from Evil and afterwards the conscience was wakened by the influence of Christ. The pattern is reflected in the growing-up of each child. He is guided in his behaviour in his early years by parents and teachers, whose word has the authority of law. He is not ready to take the whole moral responsibility for his actions himself and should be protected by obedience to the grown-ups. But when the third stage of birth is reached and he changes from a child into an independent personality, the conscience should awaken within him. He should become the judge and guardian of his own motives. In terms of the Bible, it may truly be said that a child begins life in the Old Testament and grows up into the New. The older people, who want to help him, should show him the way into the Sermon on the Mount, going from behaviour inwards to thought and feeling. The child is harmed if he is required too early to be over-conscious of his motives or even of his emotions. He will be full of fear, if he is told that what he has done has made his father or mother unhappy. The stress should be put on behaviour and its results. But if this attitude is prolonged, the young person will not be helped to develop a moral feeling in his inner life. It will harm him if the older people are satisfied when he behaves to the right pattern and are not interested in his inner impulses. "Were you good? Did you behave nicely?" The anxious parent says to the child returning from a visit. Later on the same parent will be apt to say to the youth: "How did you get on? Did they like you? Will they ask you again?" Such questions which only look to behaviour, tend to mean in reality just this: "Have you been a credit to us? Did you make yourself popular?" The inner reaction of the growing son or daughter will naturally be something like this: they don't care what I am like, but only whether I please people or not.

The conscience speaks with a spiritual voice within the soul about good and evil, about right and wrong. In one sense it speaks from experience, and may repeat at times what has been learnt from parents, teachers, ministers or people who were much admired. In a higher sense it speaks from the truth which a person wins for himself with thought and moral insight. The process of coming to an independent moral judgement is often foreshadowed by a particular experience in childhood. The child learns habits and standards from the grown-ups by obedience, but he can also react against what he disapproves of in the example they set him. The child of a bad-tempered father may resolve to learn self-control, or of a mother who cares too much for what the neighbours will say, may develop moral courage. He is able to react morally out of himself and later on in his teenage he will transform this into the power of individual conscience. His moral insight should be inspired by his imagination for ideals. He will very much need his conscience not just as a commentator but to inspire his words and actions. He can only become discontented, if he has to be an idealist in thought without performing conscientious deeds.

The conscience does two kinds of work. In the first place, it watches over the balance within the soul. How do temptations come about? It is a matter of observation to see that every impulse rising up in the soul becomes a temptation when it goes to an extreme. A prudent person, for instance, may think himself wise but if he goes too far in this direction he will become over-cautious and timid. A self-controlled person, becoming too restrained, will at last be unable to assert himself when it is necessary. But there is at the opposite extreme, a "too much" which is in contrast to the "too little" of these examples. The opposite of timidity is over-boldness, of over-restraint, no restraint at all. The over-bold person throws prudence to the winds. The unrestrained character exhausts himself in outbursts of emotion. Both fall into temptation as much as those who go into the other extreme. The good qualities are found to be in the middle, to be the balance between opposite extremes of two kinds. To be prudent is to find the mean between being bold and being timid. To be controlled is to balance out the tendency to let one's self go with that of holding one's self in. Some people are by natural character examples of one extreme or the other. There are spendthrifts and misers, fools and cowards, liars who exaggerate and liars who suppress and twist. But, in fact, the tendencies in both directions are continually influencing every-one, apart from his particular character.

"There but for the grace of God, go I" is a thought that need never be forgotten, when one realizes that each one of us is capable of every kind of bad behaviour. The tendency to swing to extremes in either direction is continually at work in every soul, bringing us into temptation against which the effort has to be made to create the balance. The swing in one direction tends to produce its opposite if too little effort is made to restrain it. Someone who has been putting up with more than he could bear, will burst into violent anger. Another, who has run away from what he feared, will take a foolhardy leap into danger. Still another who has been mean with his money over one thing will often be extravagant over the next. The conscience watches over the swinging movement in the life of the soul, that pulls from one temptation to its opposite. A person whose conscience is well awake and who listens willingly to its voice, will observe what is going on in himself and be on his guard. Self-observation of this kind is important to young people, who are in the process of learning to depend on their own powers of conscience. Instead of training themselves to ask, am I doing right, am I doing wrong, they may start with another, more inward question. They can say: what is happening in me? Do I really feel this or are my feelings running away with me and where are they running to? If I get so angry now, shall I not be bullying someone before long? If I am so greedy for that now, shall I not later hate it?

The conscience has another work to do. It watches over the temptations but it inspires the effort to create what is good between the extremes of what is bad. We experience the swing from one opposite to another, not as something brought about by ourselves, but as something that happens to us. But the balance, that which arises in the centre, is created by our own effort. That does not happen to us but we have to fashion it by bringing under our own control the forces of the soul. If I wish to have courage, I must take hold of that which is tending to make me either cowardly or foolhardy. In the centre, I must bring about courage. Shall I be generous, then I must overcome both the fear of giving and the wish to throw all I have away and produce a generous action. Can I be loving, it will be necessary for me to overcome both my own need for affection and my longing to pour my emotion over another person, and create a selfless interest in the other one to whom I wish to give love. Courage, generosity and love do not exist in me until I create them by my own will. If I remain passive, my reactions will swing from one opposite to the other and, if I follow them thoughtlessly, my behaviour will do likewise. When I am inwardly active, I can become a morally creative person, from whose centre the Good is being brought to life.

A picture for our inner life can be found in the world outside, in the moon and the sun. The moon sheds her own silvery light in the dark night sky but she is not producing it herself. Moonlight is reflected sunlight. All our human thoughts, feelings and behaviour, when they are really reactions, are like moonlight. We have thoughts that are stimulated by what we have seen and heard from outside. We react in our thinking. Feelings arise from what we experience and, left to follow their own nature, will run to extremes. So we react with our feelings and if we thoughtlessly follow our own bent, we shall behave accordingly. The soul-life becomes moonlike. But if the conscience takes a hand, it becomes sunlike. When we start to think, not only because of a reaction, but independently from within, we begin to think in ideals. They are ideas fraught with moral feeling. They shine with goodness. They are discovered from inside the mind. When we let their light shine upon our experiences, we stop simply reacting and begin to be creative. This is not done by thinking alone. It requires will. The first effort of will has to be made to control the swing of feeling from one opposite to the other. The centre-point of balance is established. The second effort of will follows, to create there by the inspiration of a moral idea, an active impulse of good. It begins to shine, to shed warmth and strength over the whole being and into the world beyond. The soul-life becomes sunlike, for the conscience is at work in thinking, feeling and willing. Goodness shines into thought and action.

In the last century there was an English queen, who inherited the throne at the age when she stood at the threshold of youth. The story is told of this young Victoria that she was called out of bed very early in the morning to receive from the Prime Minister the news that her uncle the King had died that night and that she was to be queen. It is said that she stood in the dawn facing this eminent statesman and said: "I will be good." Such simple-minded words came from the heart of a child, who had just entered youth and was encountering the destiny that life was bringing to meet her. Everyone in growing-up encounters such a moment of destiny, though in different circumstances, and longs to make this promise to himself. The impulse of the heart to be good is the birthgift we have all brought with us into this world, although we have to preserve it in the midst of manifold temptations. The Spiritual World has given us the gift and this world sends us the temptations, but the impulse to be good came first. Nevertheless when childhood has been left behind, the simple saying: "I will be good" is not enough. The nature of the human soul will not allow us to "be good". Another, more active, expression is needed. If we take here a well-known phrase and change its old meaning into a new one, we can say: "We have to make good". People who listen to the conscience are "makers of good". No one can be good without continually creating within himself goodness that will shine from his heart like the sun.

When young people nowadays reach the point where they have to make the transition from obedience to authority to listening to the voice of conscience, the experience is made the harder for them by the fact that, historically speaking, Mankind has not yet achieved it. Conscience is still regarded as part of the private life of an individual person, and law backed by force belongs to the public life. We are in a great world-dilemma today. International affairs run on something like this: our law against yours, our bombs against yours, our force against yours. There is no peace in the world, just as there would be no peace in a family that lived together on this principle, and no peace in the heart of a single person who lived like this with himself. A young person growing up into this state of affairs loses all sight of his conscience if he accepts it and adapts himself to it. But he can see a great purpose in his own inner efforts, if he recognizes the idea that he is responsible for "making good". In youth it often seems unattractive to find a ready-made world waiting for one. "Is there a contribution for me to make?" is the urgent question of many a young heart, "I don't want just to be part of the system". The answer to a question like this is found in understanding the real meaning of the conscience. My contribution starts when "I make good" in myself, but it does not stop there. The conscience is like the sun, it shines.

The thought has been put forward previously in these pages that at the present stage of history Humanity faces a decision, which is also the decision that each man and woman faces in his or her own life. There are two kinds of evolution ahead of us. Shall we rise up out of our fall into material existence, with its temptations, or shall we accept it, make much of it, and grow further into it? What is wrong with material existence, that it seems to push us on to the downward path in evolution? Why cannot we just stay as we are and enjoy our life here, while it lasts? From our own human point of view, why should we be faced at all with a great decision, either for ourselves or for Mankind? Such questions can well arise in our minds today, if we look from one side only, from the earthly. But we live between the earthly and the spiritual, both meet in us. We are partly of the earth and partly of the Spirit. How does it look from the spiritual side, in the eyes of God? One of the parables taken from the Gospel of St Luke has been quoted earlier and can be thought of again now. The son, who left his Father's house and went into the far country, took much wealth with him, which he wasted. When he tried to live off the country in which he was, he found that he must starve. He did not really belong there. He came to himself and decided to go back to the Father's house. He had to make a decision to go or to stay, to make the tremendous effort to return or sit down and starve. So our earth existence looks when seen from the Divine World. Either human beings cease to be the sons of God because they stay too long in the far country or they find the Father again, who will say: "This my son was dead and is alive again, was lost and is found." At the threshold of life, in youth the question is encountered, which we all carry with us as long as we live on earth.

V

THE CHURCH

"THAT man shouted so loud," remarked the little girl who had been taken to hear a sermon in church for the first time, "that God could have heard him, if He had been in Heaven. But God may be standing by his side." Where is God to be found? We look in three directions to find where He is present, upwards to the heavens, inwards into our own heart and outwards to the other people around. We might seem to be ignoring the modern explorations into space, if we look for the Heavens above the earth. But the stars that shine in the sky do not only represent bodies but Spirits too. Behind the outer appearance of their shining is the spiritual presence of the beings traditionally called angels, archangels and all the company of Heaven. The pattern of stars at night is the countenance which the Divine World turns to the earth, both hiding and revealing the Spirit behind it, just as our faces show to each other, or hide, our spirit. Looking inwards we recognize that divine forces are at work both in the fashioning of our body and soul and in the presence of the indwelling spirit. Thanking God for our capacities of body and soul is not a custom today. One might almost believe that people nowadays expect to have all that is given to them as a right and look for someone to blame if anything is amiss. In fact we are not self-made and ought not to forget it. Looking outwards we recognize the same divine forces at work in other people as in ourselves and we apprehend the individual divine spirit within each one. Often we see or hear of too many people to be actively sensitive to them as human divine beings. They become just a mass but those of whom we become individually aware remind us that the mass is really an illusion.

The little girl spoke wisely when she said: God is standing near us, we don't need to shout at Him from the distance. His working weaves through all our existence and we cannot if we have a sense of reality ignore it. People who lived at an earlier time in history realized this so clearly that they always built the church to be the centre of the town or the village, with a tower or spire that could be seen from the distance long before any other building came into view. This is no longer so in the West but there are parts of the world where the old feeling lives on. A visitor to London from the East asked why religion was shut away in special buildings called churches, to which people only went at certain times. Why was religion not to be noticed in the street and in the customs of daily life? A visiting student from Africa put the same problem in another question. Here in the West, she said, you are very clever. Your surgeons are so clever that they can make a dying man live three years longer than he could by himself. But what does he do with the three years? He reads the newspaper.

Children today grow up to enter the adult world and find its inhabitants beset with spiritual confusion. What, for instance, does the word "religion" mean? It is liable to many meanings, of which the most practical is the religious institution, embodied in a building and an organization, to which one does or does not belong. The boy or girl, who knows the streets of his or her town and has visited other places, sees temples, synagogues and churches, Protestant, Catholic and of other varieties. He observes them from outside and knows them apart. He will probably soon find out what they look like from inside and compare them with the place of worship to which his parents take him. In his adolescent years he can visit them while the services are on and get to learn the different forms of worship, Christian or non-Christian. Children do not benefit by being taken from one church to another, but young people, whose intellectual powers have developed, can with advantage learn about the kinds of religion practised by the people round them. The hunger for experience is strong at this period of life and needs to be satisfied by a wide diet. To visit every place of worship in the town, one after the other, is a useful piece of religious education during the last years at school. An older member of the family can go too for company or a small group of young people may go together.

The matter will not, of course, stop there. While they are still at school, the boys and girls will encounter different customs, principles and beliefs in each other's families. Where do these come from? What do they mean? Who is right? How to find the way through the confused situation? Young people have strong emotional responses to what they meet. They are attracted here and repelled there, but they can only little by little find out how to discern the value of their different experiences. This is not the time of life for deciding to belong to one religion or another. These are the years of experience, not of decision. Many parents and teachers worry more than is necessary over the phases through which young people are apt to pass. The anxious question is often put: what if he is always like he is now? why does he take a fancy to just this or that, which we most dislike? The answer, of course, lies in the fact that with young people the one sure thing is that they will not stay as they are now. The special grace given to us all in youth is to continually change and grow. But even this has a shadow, the sense of uncertainty which accompanies it and is all the worse because of the spiritual confusion in the minds of so many elder people whom the young ones encounter.

The strongest impulse in the heart of a young person is to look for an older and wiser person, whom he can trust as a guide into the adult world. He will want to choose for himself, who this shall be and he will, as it were, make his own terms. The child will accept authority, the young person will reject it, but at the very same time will be looking for someone to guide him and receive his confidence. Much bad behaviour in the years of adolescence comes from disappointment when older people worthy of trust are not to be found. The adolescents feel there should be a few who know the way through the maze of experience and can point it out to others. In matters of religion this impulse is the one most to be reckoned with during adolescence. Young people will broaden their minds by getting to know many kinds of religion and many doctrines. But it will often be an intellectual affair. Their hearts will respond to the people who represent them. They are looking for people to admire. The little child imitates, the child worships a hero, the young person trusts a guide; in such a generalization the tendency common to the different steps of growing-up can be expressed.

The person whom the boy or girl meets in youth is much more important than the religion behind him and may well determine where he or she will turn their steps for years. Parents or others who want to help will not be able to find and choose the right person. The force of an individual destiny has begun to work, which demands to be respected. There are people who try to organize valuable experiences for their children or others whom they wish to help. A play was once written about a father who tried to plan and arrange for his little daughter's first memory. Naturally he could not do so, because the child would respond, not to him, but to the impulses of her own being through which the higher wisdom, outside the range of our knowing, works.

Destiny is a force coming straight from the Divine World and does not fit in with man-made plans. How each individual finds his own spiritual experiences belongs to the deeply hidden will in him which guides him with divine wisdom. Destiny does not command or coerce but it brings the necessities, which in our lives become opportunities. One can pray for the one whom one loves but cannot plan his experiences or direct his life. This is one of the fundamental experiences, which come to parents as their children grow up. How can they let them find their own way, without leaving them quite alone? Whenever, at any time in life, one wishes to help another without interfering, one can pray for him. One's personal feeling of love can be offered to his guardian angel, who has his highest interests at heart, and the angel will weave the human love into his own light and let it shine into the soul of him for whom the prayer was offered. In such a way, the wisdom higher than one's own inspires the force of his love and more is offered than one could achieve alone. All those who bring up children and young people need skill in prayer, that their human efforts may meet and flow along with the divine will that works into the life of each one of us in the hidden stream of destiny.

The young people will have to find their way through the assortment of religious institutions that exist today. If they have learnt how to read world history in the way which was described in an earlier chapter, they will have the means of understanding what they encounter. Each of the known religions and churches has its rightful place in the pattern of history. Some were up-to-date earlier, some later in time, but each represents a stage in the religious experience of Mankind and can be understood when rightly placed in its historical setting. As the institutions are today, they are like pieces in a museum, most of them belonging to the past more than to the present stage of Mankind's life. But the young people will encounter another experience. People of many kinds, identifying religion completely with such institutions, maintain that today, Mankind has outgrown the need for God. Such an attitude is expressed in a variety of ways, from the philosophical considerations of scientific intellectuals to the primitive assertions of those Communists who make it a duty to disbelieve in God, as it was once a duty to do so. How can they know how to estimate what they meet of this kind? They will have to consult their own personal sense of reality. Much will depend on how far those who brought them up, have cultivated it and kept it clear and true in their hearts. We all have this inspired kind of common sense which allows us to see what is true behind the argument. But we do not all trust it or keep it clear of confusion. If we take an example from the sayings of Christ, we find in the Sermon on the Mount the sentence (in the old version): "Which of you by taking thought can add one cubit to his stature?" Who, in other words, can make himself grow? No answer follows in the Sermon on the Mount, because, put like that, none is needed. The sense of reality supplies it and will be able to give other answers to other questions.

It is a matter of common sense which can be made quite clear in the religious education of children and young people, that religion and religious institutions are not the same thing. Christianity, for instance, is not to be identified with the many churches devoted to its cause. It is greater than them all, a world-force in evolution, as Shelley has described it in his poem "Hellas".

> "A Power from the unknown God,
> A Promethean Conqueror came;
> Like a triumphal path he trod
>   The thorns of death and shame.

A mortal shape to him
Was like the vapour dim
Which the orient planet animates with light.
Hell, sin and slavery came
Like bloodhounds mild and tame
Nor preyed until their Lord had taken flight.
The moon of Mahomet
Arose and it shall set
While, blazoned as on heaven's immortal noon
The cross leads generations on."

All the criticisms that can be made of churches in the past or the present, do not really touch Christianity itself. It is far more than one religion among many. Being a world-force, it can flow through churches and even religions, leaving some of its water in the pools and river-beds they provide. It is the living water in our earthly life without which it becomes parched and dry. Christianity is the world-power of Resurrection, by which Man's destiny on earth can be carried to meet the Spiritual World again. We know it because we see its working. Why are some people not crushed by suffering, but prove able to draw from it wisdom and strength? Why have some of the great failures in history borne fruit, while the successes quickly passed away? Why have those who do wrong still the power, if they will, to change and do good where they did harm? Why does weakness make us compassionate, pain gentle and helplessness kind? Why when we are so easily able to hate, do we long to give and receive love? Why when everything material is so real to us, are we dissatisfied until we feel the truth of the Spirit? Why is death not the end of everything? Why have we in our hearts forgiveness, that magic power of transformation, which turns injury into understanding, the will to destroy into the will to build up, hate into love? In all these things we are seeing the power of the Resurrection.

Jesus Christ walked on earth with His disciples. They followed Him, but how little they understood! What poor figures they cut in many of the stories! What a climax of tragedy came at Easter when one betrayed Him, one denied Him, and the rest, all but John, deserted Him! But after the deed on the Cross, in the time of the Resurrection, He came to them, to all but Judas who had hanged himself, and blessed them. They were His true disciples in those days and, receiving at Pentecost the Holy Spirit, they became the bold founders of the Christian Church. The contrast between the timorous, uncertain men who were the disciples before Easter and the heroic, clear-sighted fathers of the Church whom they became, is the measure of the power of Resurrection at work in them.

Christianity is more than one religion among others, and more than the faith of any or all the Christian churches. Such a vision is needed by young people if they are to comprehend the religious situation in the world today, and find their way through it. Does this mean that all religions and churches are of equal value, or, conversely, that none have any value today? Certainly a church or religious community as such is valuable because the religious life should not be entirely private and individual but should be shared with a community. In a Christian sense, the words of Christ can be quoted: "Where two or three are gathered together, I am in the midst." Outside Christianity the religious life tends to be even more strongly an affair of the community. Just young people, who are often very much aware of what they mean to themselves, should learn to see the right counterpart to their individual spiritual life in what is shared in a community. On principle, the Church or institution of a like kind is right and necessary. In practice, however, scarcely any part of modern society is so apt to be old-fashioned in thought and style. as the Church. New ways of coming together for spiritual purposes need to be found today. Dogma is out of place for people with modern minds who rightly feel a duty to think for themselves. Organization is very often overdone, leading to overstress on who does or who does not belong. Too much social activity can drive the spiritual into the background until the "clubby, chubby church" comes about. It would be necessary to return to fundamentals, and ask what the Church is originally and essentially meant to be.

A picture was once painted by Raphael, which describes the first idea of the Church among the early Christians. It is one of the series of illustrations to the Acts of the Apostles, painted at the order of a Pope in Rome as designs for tapestries, and which came to rest in a London gallery. The picture shows the giving of gifts of food to the Church and the distribution to the poor and needy. At its centre is painted a small platform of raw wood raised on two steps and surrounded except for the opening by a simple rail. The Apostles and deacons stand on the platform. From the right come people with sacks of corn to put as gifts on the steps. On the left others are kneeling, who receive the food from the deacon. The original Greek word for the Church meant just what is seen here, a community with a fence round it. The fence is not for protection, it does not shut anyone out, nor keep anyone in. It marks a boundary, outwardly weak, inwardly of great power. The inner forces of wisdom and courage are needed to cross it. In the picture it is very clear that not all those present, not even when they can give or receive, feel able to enter. Those on the platform stand very upright, those outside the fence are bent down under the weight of the sacks or are kneeling to receive what is given. In the contrast between their attitudes, the inner strength is described that is necessary to stand inside the Church. But the holy food is being distributed which will bring the uprightness into the being of those who receive. They will have the opportunity, when they feel able to take it, of climbing the two steps to the platform and being received within the fence. There is a very distinct difference between those outside and those inside, not imposed from without but chosen from within.

In the Old Testament we hear of the Noah's Ark, where the small group of people were collected, who were to survive the destruction of their own epoch of history and become the seed for the next. In the Acts of the Apostles we read of the Church enclosed in the fence, into which the early Christians entered through baptism and of which they became members through confirmation. In one sense they were entering a new kind of ark in which they would be rescued from the decline and fall of the ancient world. As they were received, they renounced the world, the flesh and the devil, powers very real to them, from which they were escaping. In another sense, they were entering the spiritual place where the seed of the future was planted and was to be cultivated, not for a new epoch but of the whole coming evolution of Mankind. They were carrying within them the beginnings of the new man, the upright one, who was to be born out of the power of the Resurrection.

The true Church is the community of those drawn together by recognizing the Resurrection at work in themselves and each other. If we look again at the parable of the Prodigal Son, we would say: those who have come to themselves and decided to go back to the Father's house, take the road together helping each other along. In that parable, as in all to be read in the Gospels, there is a second picture hidden behind the outer words. In this second silent picture, there is another brother, not he who would not go into the feast, but one who had not stayed at home but who had gone to find the lost one, starving in a far country. This silent figure can be felt standing behind the despairing one in the hour when he comes to himself and going with him, strengthening him on the road. He is the divine brother of Man, Christ, who has brought in Himself to earth the power to lift Mankind out of spiritual darkness and death into light and life. He is the giver of the Resurrection, who inspires all true religion today, whatever outward form it may take.

Older people, whether parents, teachers or whoever they are, cannot spare the young people they love their own experience and pain, nor can they make them from outside into Christians, or into good religious people. They may be tempted to try to do more than they should or can. But much they can do. They can show them the meaning of religion in human life today. They can steadfastly go ahead themselves in the way of Resurrection. They can be at hand to help, when the younger ones, coming behind, need picking up or helping along. A companionship can grow which, however it outwardly appears, is inspired by the real community of the Spirit. Together they can seek the true meeting of God with Man at the end of the road, to which the words belong: "For this my son was dead and is alive again, was lost and is found."

EPILOGUE

THE CHURCH TODAY

THE description of the true Church in the foregoing chapter does not apply to an institution but to the spiritual community of Christ, which comes to life here whenever and wherever "two or three gathering together in His name" is a reality. But there are people today who, finding all the established religious communities too old-fashioned and rigid, have united to build a modern Christian Church, which would recognize the wide world-embracing nature of Christianity. Outwardly, it was founded in 1922, with the inspiration and guidance of Rudolf Steiner to whom we today owe the clearest exposition of Christianity as "a religion but more than all religions" (Rudolf Steiner). The principles of the "Christian Community" as this movement is called, came from the picture of Christianity in world-evolution, which has been outlined in these pages. It is felt by many that traditions and usages from earlier times in history limit too much the possibility of the old institutions to represent Christianity in its widths and depths. To return to an earlier picture, the Christian river of life flows through history but the pools and river-beds offered us in the old institutions are too restricted to contain it. A new river-bed was needed and, although no claims are made for the Christian Community as a body to provide this, the aim of those who join it is to offer as wide and deep a one as they can make. There is no dogma in the Christian Community but each minister and member is responsible for his own thinking. Seven Sacraments in modern wording give to all who take part the common experience in the spirit, out of which the Community is formed. The spiritual processes, which take place in the Sacraments are, as they have been in the Christian Church from the beginning, the working of the power of the Resurrection in and through us. Children are cared for in the Christian Community in the way recommended in these pages.

The movement of the Christian Community is new, pioneer in character, and not yet large in numbers. But it is represented in many different countries and places in the world. All who would be interested to get to know it are welcome to find their nearest centre of its work and "come and see". There never was nor will be a better way of finding out and judging for one's self than the old and simple advice: "Come and see."